# SPENNYMOOR REMEMBERED BOOK – 4

**This book is for Josie**

## OLD PALS

**WORKS AND RESERVOIR COTTAGES 1940's**
Jack and Teresa Ainsley, Patty Brown and Freda Thompson

**BROOM STREET AND FENWICK STREET**
Doreen and Rita Williams, Joan and Marlene Hetherington

# SPENNYMOOR REMEMBERED BOOK – 4

*Compiled by*
**Bob Abley**

**ARB PUBLICATIONS**

First Published in 2003

Published by
ARB Publications
98 Durham Road
Spennymoor
County Durham
DL16 6SQ


ISBN 09536315 4 0


Printed in Great Britain by
Macdonald Press
Spennymoor
County Durham

# Contents

# Acknowledgements

Once again I have been given help by many people in the compilation of this book. I am most grateful for the time, information and material freely and generously given. I would particularly like to thank the following people:

Mrs. Richardson, Mrs. Hood, Mrs. Morgan, Betty Waugh, Sandra Stow, Anne Keane, Kim Robinson, Heather Casson, Mrs. Owens, Freda Donahoe, Julia Thompson, Vera Brydon, Mr. Marsden, Mr. Partington, Alan and Sheila Deniss, Neil and June Kelly, Ken and Margaret Appleby, Tom Cornish, Freddy Simpson, Harry Spence, Derek Wilson, Alan Spence, George Savage, Barry Easter, Tom Ward, Reg Hughes, Colin Ryder, Durham University Library and Bill Kitching.

Any mistakes are down to yours truly.

**SPENNYMOOR OVER SIXTIES TRIP c. 1950**

# Foreword

Well the last couple of years have flown over and the photographs and information keep coming in. I have a wonderful archive of photographs and conversations that I have gathered over the last few years. There are still parts of the town that are not very well covered. I would like to get more street photographs particularly of those streets that no longer exist such as those in Low Spennymoor and Merrington Lane. Also of Catherine Street, Queen Street, Duncombe Street, Villiers Street and Zion Street. I have very few photographs of Durham Road Secondary Modern School pupils from the early years surely there must be some in existence.

Over the last couple of years there have been changes in the town, two or three of our local landmarks have been demolished or are being demolished, the old Tower Brewery building that had been used by Raines the Coachbuilders and sadly North Road School, who would ever have thought it? Middlestone Moor School has also bitten the dust it makes you wonder if there are going to be any old and interesting buildings left in Spennymoor. It is just as well that people do take photographs to remind us what it was like in earlier days. These sites have been earmarked for building land and indeed one has already been developed. You ask the question, "Who is going to live in all these new houses?" but there doesn't seem to be any shortage of buyers. All of this building is on brownfield sites but the next lot of houses (800?) to be built at Whitworth are going to take another great chunk out of our countryside.

It has been pleasing to see the arrival of Peacocks in the town centre and people are looking forward to the imminent arrival of the new Farm Foods store, both of these should give a boost to the town centre. Great efforts are being made to make the town centre a better place, it is currently about to have a facelift which will hopefully attract more shoppers. There seems to be a climate of interest in improving the Town Centre which has in part been generated by the Town Forum. There are a lot of people who are interested in improving Spennymoor and this is the place to air your views. The meetings are held on a regular basis and are well advertised. It is also pleasing to see the arrival of a proper restaurant in the town, the Indian Restaurant on King Street which by all accounts is excellent; we could do with more of this sort of enterprise to liven up the town at night.

## MORE OLD PALS

**PEARSON STREET AREA C. 1953**

Photograph taken in 25 Pearson Street in the house of Aunt Bella Gooding whose head is unfortunately missing.

**Among others:** Rita Westgarth, Ann Joyce, Carol Westgarth, Jean Buckland, Pam Druit, Judith Abley, Carol Buckland, , Margaret Joyce and Hazel Abley. Aunt Kitty Brooks is on the left and her married daughter Doreen on the right

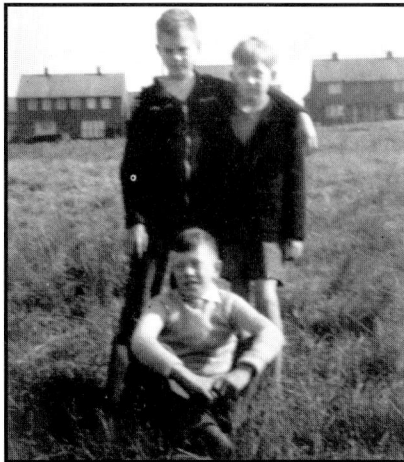

**HALFMOON LANE**
Alan Megeson, Tony Burns and Alan Hunter

# ONE

# IN AND AROUND TOWN

**THE BLACK HORSE INN c. 1962**

On the left in the triangle of land formed by the junction of Tudhoe Lane and the main road is M. Whites House the Gables. This house had previously been a farm.

**THE ARCADIA BUS STAND.**

The photograph above and the six following were taken sometime during the late 1950's by Clifford Casson. Most of them seem to have been taken on the same bleak and rainy day.

The Arcadia bus stand used to be the terminus for several bus services that served the town. The double - decker standing at the stop is Shaw's which did the Spennymoor Byers Green run. Other services which used this terminus were, Jewitt's which did the Spennymoor Page Bank run and the United services, 2, 3 and 15. The No. 2 ran between Ferryhill Station and Bishop Auckland via Spennymoor, Kirk Merrington and Chilton, the No. 3 ran between Ferryhill and Spennymoor via Half Moon Lane and the No. 15 was the Spennymoor to Darlington service.

The photograph was taken from the vantage point of the entrance to Catherine Street, bottom Doggart's corner to be exact. Directly across the road the building behind the bus is the old Wesleyan school rooms. The lower wooden building to the front of this was the Methodist Institute which housed two full sized billiard tables and a table tennis table.

The road between the Arcadia Cinema and the school rooms is Works Road. This road used to be the main entrance into the Weardale Iron and Steel Works. Looking along the road into the middle distance, on the left, is St. John's Ambulance room and in the far distance Reservoir Cottages.

**CHEAPSIDE LOOKING TOWARD HIGH STREET.**

**HIGH STREET LOOKING TOWARD THE BRIDGE.**

The white building on the left housed the National Provincial Bank on the ground floor and the Town Hall Cinema on the first floor. In the distance the Eden bus can be seen pulling away from the Vane Arms Bus Stop (The Bridge) on its way to Shildon and West Auckland.

**SPENNYMOOR BRIDGE BUS STOP**

**THE VANE ARMS BUS STOP.**
Showing the Surtee's pub, Blaylock's the photographers, Wise's fish shop and the
Wheatsheaf pub.

**CARR LANE.**

This was before the Yuill estate was built and as can be seen the road is in a state of disrepair. On the left can be seen Whitworth Colliery pit heaps and part of the colliery railway sidings.

**THE TOWN HALL BUILDINGS**

An unusual shot taken from the railway station. The white building is the Town Hall Cinema with the projection box sticking out at the back

**COULSON STREET 1915**

On the left Mount Pleasant Infant school which had opened in 1912 and the large building looming in the background the Weardale Street Methodist Chapel. In the right foreground is the post office and following the run of buildings into the distance, are among other businesses, the Tudhoe Co-op, The Puddlers Arms, the Vulcan Inn, Andrew Hall the Grocer, and the Golden Fleece Inn

**COULSON STREET c.1970**

On the left in the foreground is the only remaining part of the Weardale Iron and Steel works, part of the wall that was built along the Coulson Street side of the works, it remains to this day. On the right the little petrol station belonging to Ernie Brooks who was tragically killed in an accident in his gyrocopter. Then the Iron Works pub starts the run of shops and businesses which terminates with the Golden Fleece pub in the distance.

**HIGH WHITWORTH FARM c. 1965.**

This farm was on land owned by the Shafto family and it was adjacent to Whitworth Park Colliery. During the 1920's the farm was rented from the Shaftos by John Gornall who had been the groom at Whitworth Hall. Mr. Gornall farmed the land and had a milk business in Spennymoor. He later started to lead coals from Whitworth Colliery and this business later developed into a road haulage firm which carried loads of bricks to all parts of the country. This business was eventually taken over by his son John who ran it until his recent retirement. The house has of course been modernised and extended and stands in open countryside now that Whitworth Colliery no longer exists but, if recent plans go ahead the house could find itself surrounded by a new housing estate of up to 800 houses.

**DEMOLITION OF WOOLWORTH 1968**

The shop was demolished to make way for the widening of Oxford Road to take the traffic away from the town centre and the main shopping area.

**DERELICT AREA.**

This is the area earmarked for the building of the shopping centre. The streets demolished were Catherine Street, Duncombe Street, Villiers, Street, Zion Street and Oxford Street. The Zion Chapel is left standing as is one side of Zion Street and a small part of Villiers Street. The road leading to nowhere on the left, once opened into Catherine Street. The photograph was taken from a newspaper article in 1964 headlined **"BLITZ! The attack will be on bad housing, dereliction and poor roads. It will be on Spennymoor, Spennymoor will be a showplace."**

**CATHERINE STREET AREA 1946.**

A pencil drawing by Robert Heslop in 1942 showing the streets in the area as they were before the demolition that had taken place in the photograph above.

**ONE OF THE CASUALTIES OF THE REGENERATION OF THE TOWN CENTRE**

After nearly 80 years in business in the town Mr. Walls the son of the founder said that he could not afford to take one of the new units on the shopping precinct and therefore had no alternative than to close the business.

### OTHER VICTIMS OF PROGRESS

**Foundry Street, Merrington Lane.** These houses had once been the Railway Hotel but prior to demolition they had been private houses. The land was compulsorily purchased for urgent industrial development (a car park}. The whole village was demolished apart from the Steam Mill pub (now the Winning Post).

# SPENNYMOOR REMEMBERED – BOOK 4

## THE FAR-REACHING CHANGES THAT TOOK PLACE IN THE TOWN DURING THE 1960'S.

After the Second World War Spennymoor was desperately in need of regeneration, there was a need for more jobs and the replacement of old and unsanitary housing. The coalmining industry was running down and new industries needed to be attracted to the area. Housing had always been a problem in Spennymoor right from its very beginnings; there were never enough houses for the people that needed them. By 1947 the Royal Ordnance Factory, built during the war, had closed down and the site was being developed by Siemens Brothers, Smart and Brown (engineers) and T.Summerson & Sons Ltd. Also by 1947 an ambitious housing programme was underway, houses being built by the Council and the North East Housing Association in several parts of the town. Even so the waiting list at the time was well over 1000 and there was always a waiting list into the hundreds up to the early 1960's.

Despite this progress the nature of the town remained the same but big changes were in the offing these being sparked off by the Hailsham Report of 1963. Spennymoor was to become a growth zone along with Newton Aycliffe and Darlington. Every effort was to be made to attract new industry to the area and with this in mind Spennymoor was to be connected to the new Durham motorway by an efficient system of roads and the Merrington Lane and Thinford industrial sites were to be expanded.

When the Hailsham Report was discussed by the Town Council at a meeting in December 1963 Councillor Thompson said that Spennymoor had plans for improving the centre of the town, a new post Office, bus station and important shopping facilities. Also he said that Spennymoor had something that was rather rare in the North East, a vast open space in the centre of the town, the old Ironworks site of 79 acres. He went on to say that the Town Council had been told that the development of this area must be planned with exceptional care because the planning of it could decide the future of Spennymoor. He stated that the council had already had expert opinion on this and were busy considering how it should be planned. Councillor Kitson said that there would be lots of loopholes and loose ends but it was a start and has set the ball rolling to improving the town.

By June 1964 Durham County Council were seeking to make Spennymoor a showcase for what could be done in regenerating the County. Since the war massive sums of money had been spent in Durham County on new houses, new schools and new roads. Despite this results had been disappointing because the new developments were scattered among the remnants of the old, derelict mines, unsightly pit heaps, old poor housing and down at heel groups of shops. What Durham County Council were seeking to do in Spennymoor was to telescope the work of two decades into 2 years, hence the newspaper headline "Spennymoor Blitz."

The Spennymoor plan was an effort to make a breakthrough, to do everything that needed to be done in a particular area and when it was done it would be possible to say that this is what County Durham could be. If it could be done in Spennymoor it can be done elsewhere in the County. It would be crash programme that would be a pilot scheme to demonstrate the regeneration of an urban environment.

Mr. Atkinson the County Planning Officer had the following observations to make: The standards of design, amenity and accommodation would condition for good or bad, the economic and social future of the whole town. It is not enough that the development should be visually attractive and exciting; care must also be taken to ensure that the type of accommodation provided will be of a standard acceptable to a future and more prosperous generation and that it is tailored to meet the needs of the people who will live in it. Mr. Atkinson was emphatic about the place of the car in the new Spennymoor. "Traffic must be kept out of the central shopping area."

Thus the plans for the building of the Bessemer park housing estate and the construction of the new town centre Parkwood Precinct were put in motion and by 1971 most of the building work had been completed. Parkwood Precinct was built and owned by Arndale Shopping Centres of Leeds and the contract for building Bessemer Park went to Concrete (Northern ) Limited who were manufacturers of Bison precast floors, roofs and high wall systems for houses, flats and car parks.

## OFFICIAL OPENING OF BESSEMER PARK ESTATE 16TH MAY 1969

Anthony Greenwood Minister of Housing officially opened Bessemer Park. He said that the project had given a new heart to Spennymoor. It was a 43 acre site and would eventually have 1009 dwellings. The estate provides flats and single and double storey houses and 70% of the dwellings would be at ground level.

The site was almost traffic free though no house was more than half a minute's walk from a car park or service area. It cost £3,730,000 to build and another £95,000 was set aside for a school and a youth club.

**ANTHONY GREENWOOD OFFICIALLY OPENING BESSEMER PARK**

**BESSEMER PARK c. 1971**
Note the old railway embankment in the fore ground. The tower blocks are far from being visually attractive and exciting.

## PEDESTRIANISING THE TOWN CENTRE

In 1972 the Urban district council along with Durham County Council prepared a report on the town centre. One of the problems revealed by the report was:
"The continued use of the High Street and Cheapside by "through" and local traffic makes conditions for shoppers unpleasant and sometimes dangerous and contributes to congestion at the junction of Barnfield Road and King Street. This problem will become more acute with the expected future growth in car ownership and development of new projects on both sides of these roads. The only effective solution is the exclusion of traffic from the shopping streets.

The Councils' suggestion was that traffic would be excluded from the main shopping areas in Cheapside and part of the High street, creating a traffic free area linking shops on both sides of the High street and Cheapside as well as the Health Centre, Library and the proposed Sports centre. Vehicular traffic would be rerouted along an extension of Oxford Road into King Street This plan was to be completed in two stages

### Stage 1
Cheapside and High street were to be closed to traffic between King William Street and Thomas Street for an experimental period of at least 6 months when Oxford Road had been extended to King Street. During the experiment buses would operate from the existing bus station

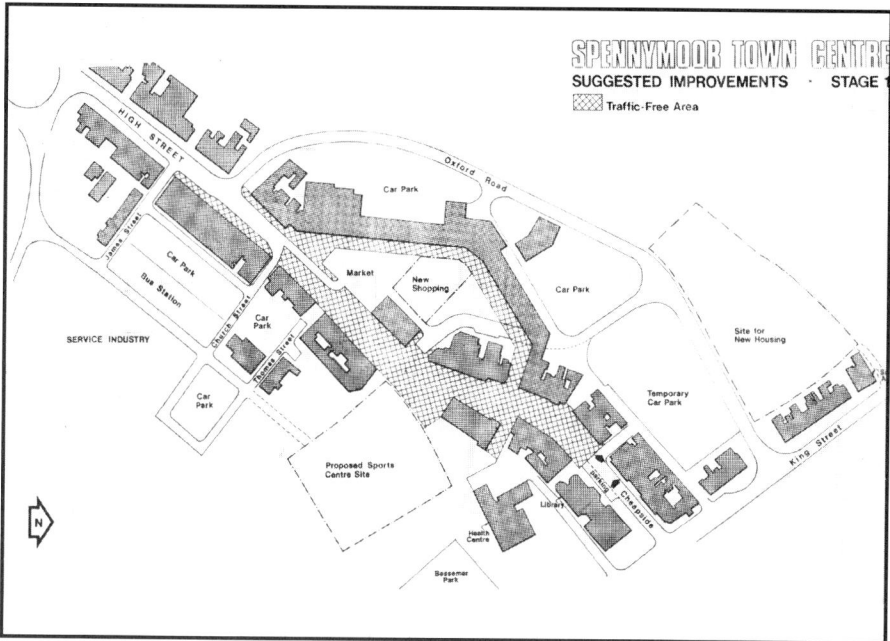

**Stage 1**

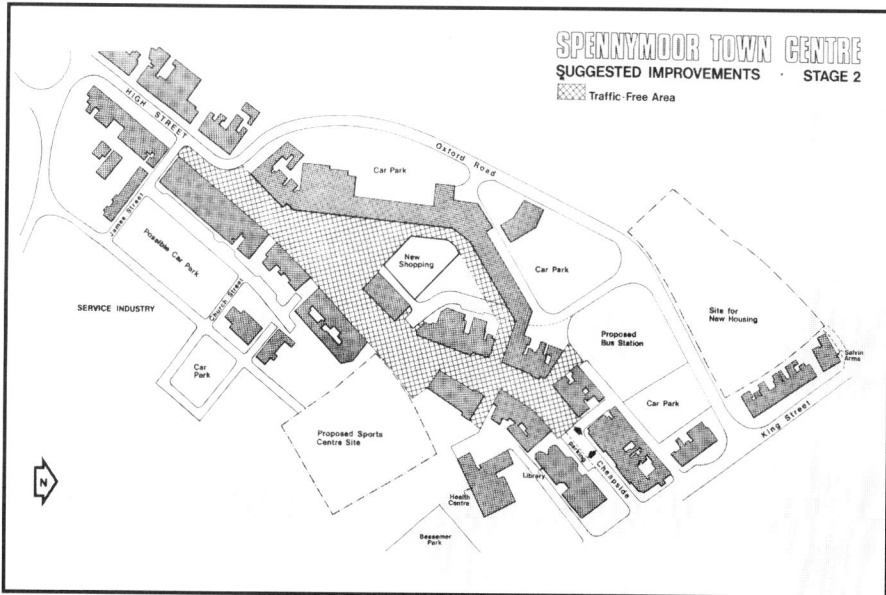

**Stage 2**

## Stage 2

If the experimental scheme was successful a permanent enclosure order would be made. The bus station would be moved and the car park in front of Parkwood Precinct would be discontinued and would become the town square. Permanent landscaping and floorscaping would be provided in the whole of the pedestrian area.

**PARKWOOD PRECINCT 1971**

## DO YOUR SHOPPING
in Safety and Comfort
AT SPENNYMOOR

## Visit the New
## SHOPPING ARCADE

Attractive Stall Units

Underfloor Heating

Toilet Facilities

● FREE CAR PARKS ●

Shopping of the Future
TODAY!

● ● ●

Enquiries for Stalls and Cafeteria to :—

**CLERK OF THE COUNCIL
TOWN HALL, SPENNYMOOR**
Tel.: Spennymoor 2302

MODERN SHOPPING SERVICE
IN THE
## CENTRAL ARCADE

### PEGGY'S
Prop.: E. SNOWBALL
OF KING STREET
FOR
Ladies Fashions
●
Costume Jewellery
●
Knitting Wools

XMAS CAKES & MINCE PIES
### H. & M. BAKERIES
Tel. FERRYHILL 416
Prop.: W. R. Proudfoot

● CREAM CAKES ●

● PIES AND PASTIES ●
● BREAD ●
SCONES & BREAD ROLLS
FRESH DAILY

### HYGIENIC FISHERIES
Prop. : D. HIGGINS

OUR MOTTO
CLEANLINESS ● QUALITY
● CIVILITY ●
NORTH SHIELDS SUPPLIES
FRESH DAILY

Call on us and choose from our
Large Variety of Fish.
PRIME LEMON SOLE PLAICE
HALIBUT, ETC.

### J. & F.
★ BLYTHE ★
FRESH FARM PRODUCE

EGGS ● CURDS
CHEESE ● BUTTER
FRUIT & VEGETABLES

ORDERS NOW FOR
XMAS POULTRY

### ALISON'S
Prop.: G. WEARMOUTH

For Ideal
CHRISTMAS GIFTS
The Latest in
FANCY GOODS
★ TOYS ★
AND NOVELTIES

### CROFT BROS.
FOR
ALL HOUSEHOLD
GOODS
AT CUT PRICES
Dettol 3/11 ● Steradent 3/6
Wonder Set 4/11 ● Dyox 1/-
Min Spray 3/11 ● Harpic 2/3
Imperial Leather 2 for 2/9

BIG SAVINGS ON TOOTHPASTES
AND MANY MORE GOODS

## GUY & HANSELMAN
BEEF & PORK BUTCHERS
PERSONAL SERVICE :: GUARANTEED SATISFACTION
Tel. SPENNYMOOR 3319

**ADVERT FOR THE INDOOR MARKET NOVEMBER 1966**

## PRIVATE HOUSING DEVELOPMENT

As Council housing development moved on apace there was also the development of private housing estates in Spennymoor for the first time.

**The Greenways Estate.** This was a development by Cecil Yuill Limited and planned to provide 700 houses. The advert below, the top part which is missing, was aiming to stress the point that it was just as cheap to buy as it was to rent.

**Middlestone Moor.** This was a development in South View by H. F. Johnson of Hurworth

The prices are certainly eye watering compared with today

**Tudhoe Grange:** This was a site of 24 acres most of which was going to be developed by Moore and Cartwright the remainder divided into individual plots for people to build to their own design. The site was eventually taken over by Wimpey Limited and became the Grange Estate,

Most of the information regarding the regeneration of Spennymoor came from various sources. Numerous newspaper cuttings probably from, The Northern Echo, Evening Despatch or the Auckland Chronicle; a handout published by Spennymoor Urban District Council and the Town Guide for 1970. I am indebted to Mrs. Morgan of Willington for the use of her scrap books and also to Mr. and Mrs. Alan Dennis for the use of the scrapbooks which belonged to Alan's father.

**THE OLD TOWER BREWERY 1970**

Originally built by Mr. Ogleby around 1871, the water for the brewing process came from a well behind Wood Vue but as the population of Spennymoor grew the well became contaminated and the brewery was closed. It was later taken over by Mr. Junor of Durham. The premises were then taken over by the North Eastern Breweries Limited; the faint outline of the name can still be seen on the roof. The last owners of the premises were Raines the coachbuilder, the building was demolished earlier this year to make way for old folk's homes.

# TWO

# SCHOOLS

The following two photographs are taken from a whole school panoramic photograph of the Alderman Wraith School taken in 1929.

## 1929

Spring Term saw the addition of new buildings. "the new labs. in the boy's yard were opened this term. There was a rumour that the old labs were going to be turned into a gymnasium, surely one of the crying needs of the School." The rumour was unfounded; the new gymnasium, with other buildings was only begun ten years later, remained unfinished due to the exigencies of war, and was incomplete when the Alderman Wraith School moved to its new quarters in 1954, the year in which "the new labs." Of 1929 were destroyed by fire.

This year the School play was a comedy by Tolstoy, "the Fruits of Enlightenment."

86 candidates sat for the Oxford Certificate and 72 candidates were awarded. A new policy was inaugurated for the Higher examination: the Arts students continued to take the Oxford Higher (8 sat, 2 were awarded); the science students took the Durham Higher (8 sat, 5 were awarded). Of the latter Alex Barraclough won a State Scholarship.

Extracted from A Jubilee History 1912 – 1962

## SCHOOL HOWLERS

The zebra is a sort of cream-coloured donkey with black stripes from which they make grate polish.

They gave the Duke of Wellington a lovely funeral. It took six men to carry the beer.

Barbarians are things put in a bicycle wheel to make it run smoothly.

Poetry is when every line begins with a capital letter.

G. Howe Upper 5d.

## Alderman Wraith Soccer Team 1929 – 39

T. Blair, J. Stanworth, E. Pratt, W. Hetherington, J. Phillips, W. Clark, G.L.Leake, W.A. Simpson (Capt.), W.Foster, F.W. Cleig, and D. Curry.

The 1929-30 season proved exceptionally fortunate for the School 1$^{st}$. X1. Twenty games were played, of which we won thirteen, lost five and drew two. Although the phenomenal scoring of last season was not equalled, the school was not far behind in this respect. The causes of the School's great success are not far to seek. The team was changed but little throughout the whole season, and so was able to show excellent combination and fine team spirit. Moreover, in Simpson the School had an excellent captain; popular, and well able to infuse his own optimism and confidence throughout the whole team.

The principal scorers were Foster, who scored 24 goals; Simpson with 23; and Leake, with 17. New caps were awarded to Foster, Phillips, Pratt, Leake, Clark and Curry. Simpson, Hetherington and Blair were given renewals.

Total Goals: - For, 90; Against, 38

F.L., Secretary.

Extracted from The Wraith Magazine July 1930

**Cartoons of the Alderman Wraith School Football X1 1929-30.**
**1929-30 Soccer Team.**

The School First Eleven has met with outstanding success this season. To what is it due? Below are candid criticisms by – does it matter?

**Goal: T. Blair.**  A good goalkeeper but somewhat erratic. He effects some wonderful saves, and then loses confidence – by "muffing" a simple shot, stick to football "Doole."

**Rt. Back: J. Stanworth.**  A hard worker but we expect greater things from him – it can be said in his favour that he is out of his position - is never modest in voicing his opinions.

**Left Back: E. Pratt.**  Can be relied on – is undoubtedly the best full -back in the school.

**Rt. Half-Back: W. Hetherington.**  Probably the best half-back in the school – really clever with his head, but his clearances are rather week – has played some outstanding games.

**Centre Half-Back:  J. Phillips.**  Quite a good player – uses his weight to advantage but lacks finesse – a trier will improve.

**Left Half-Back: W. Clark.**  A wholehearted player. He tends to be slow – is a terrific shot with left foot but rather weak with his right.

**Outside Right: G.L.Leake.** A good player but recent performances somewhat disappointing – has never reached his top form – capable of better things – possibly at inside position.

**Inside Right: W.A.Simpson.** The captain of the team, - brilliant at times – always loath to part with the ball – ties opposition (and himself) into knots – possible scoring chances wasted as his colleagues do not know what he is going to do.

**Central Forward: W. Foster.** A reliable player and a good shot – top scorer with 24 – 'nuff said.

**Inside left: F.D.Gleig.** The newcomer of the team – tricky, but is much too slow – quicken up Gleig, and then-

**Outside Left: D.Curry.** The smallest player on the team. A good player and can be brilliant when he exerts himself – but when does he do so?

**Alderman Wraith Hockey Team 1929-30**

Betty Raine, Esther Benfold, Cathie Gleig (Captain), Florrie James, Linda Edwards, Maggie Smare, Bertha Hornsby, Bessie Swinbank, Evelyn Stanworth, Beatrice Wheeler and Mary Keers.

The hockey team had a fairly successful season. Unfortunately we again were beaten by Chester-le-Street in the first league match of the season and so dropped out. Fixtures were obtained for almost every Saturday of the season but many of them were cancelled owing to the inclemency of the weather.

Hockey colours were awarded to for the first time last season to Eleanor Snowdon, May Hails, Mollie Taylor, Maggie Smare, Lily Steel and Katherine Gleig.

This season colours were awarded to Bertha Hornsby, Esther Benfold, Bessie Swinbank, Florrie James and Evelyn Stanworth.

**Played 15, Won 6, Lost 7 and Drawn 2**

Extracted from The Wraith Magazine July 1930.

**King Street School Football Team 1953-53.**
**Back row:** G. Hepple, J.Lowes, T. Fitzgerald, W. Illingworth, H. Healey, N. Bulmer
**Front row:** Teacher W. Nunn, J. Waterhouse, K. Brain, I. Miller, B. Milburn.

**King Street Boys Class 4 1950**
**Back row:** Cant, Testo, Batey, Denham, Carr, Scarlet, Bear, Lowes, Milburn, Waterhouse, Johns and Dargue.
**3rd row:** Scollard, Hood, Treggoning, Miller, Illingworth, Sleep, Whitehead, Cook, Brain, Pumford, Saines and Bell.
**2nd row:** Smails, Bramwell, Watchman, Welsh, Cowans (teacher), Fairhurst, Healey, Graham, Biddle and Cook.
**Front row:** Myers, Rennison, Bacon, Wilson, Foster, Snowball, Fitzgerald and Tatham.

**Class 7 Girls King Street School 1950**
**Among others:** Janet Barker, Vera Johnson, Betty Foster, Joyce Bell, Margaret Cooper, Eva Johns, Rose Appleby, Doris Wilson, Margaret Hopper, Catherine Geldart, Anne Whitehead, Freda Thompson, Ruby Fairless, Pauline Rennison, Freda Kirkby, Dorothy Spowart, Shirley Whitehouse and Jean Curry. The teacher is Gloria Gray.

**ROSA STREET SCHOOL GIRLS 1961**
**Back Row:** Christine Norman, Pamela Anthony, Ann Nelson, Linda bell, Jean Campbell and Margaret Robson.
**Middle Row:** Susan Mellor, Janice Turner, Miss Elmes, Heather Casson and Christine Kitson.
**Front Row:** Jane Mattison, Jill Sellers, Kathleen Ince, Janice Holgarth, Vicky Harris, Rita Russel and Pat Smith.

**ROSA STREET SCHOOL HARVEST FESTIVAL c. 1952**
**Among others:** Keith and Christine Wearmouth, Pat Rooney, George Smith, Terry Robson, David Mackintosh, Neil Morgan, Neil Adams and Jimmy Suddes.

**MIDDLESTONE MOOR SCHOOL WOODWORK ROOM**
**Among others;** John Blaylock and Alan Deniss.

TUDHOE COLLIERY SCHOOL 1910 – CLASS 8

TUDHOE COLLIERY SCHOOL 1920 – CLASS 3

**TUDHOE COLLIERY SCHOOL 1930**

**Back Row:** Mrs. Shill, Jim Swainston, Robert Brown, Jack Deacon, Albert Thompson, Fred Urwin, Bill Boden, Claude Strophair, Tom Pennick, George Riggins, Harold Wregglesworth, Dennis Gittins, Roy Scurr, Ernest Smart, Stan Snowball and Tom Clarehaugh.

**Front Row:** Elsie Bainbridge, Gladys Sokell, Jenny Storey, Gladys Ferguson, Vera Rowcroft, Bessie Burden, Elsie Warren, Carrie Kay, Bella Turner, Dora Kitching, Mary Pendel, Iris Swales and Joyce Clew.

**NORTH ROAD GIRLS 1928**

**NORTH ROAD GIRLS SCHOOL STAFF**

Among others: Mrs. Tuck, Miss Fishburn, Miss Simpson, Mrs. Craik, Miss Kirk, Miss Wilson, Miss Hedley and Miss Rowe.

**NORTH ROAD GIRLS CLASS 1**

**Back Row among others:** Mary Birchall, Ivy Irwin, Lillian Shearer, Daphne Harper, Freda Hills, Jean Stansby, Brenda Cardy, Margaret Langham and Norma Tanner.

**Middle Row:** Pat Corner, Olwyn Parry, Jean Stapleton, Heather Burke, Norma Rivers, Vera Russell, Rose Ebdon, Marie Hodgson, Olga Reed, Margaret Spence and Mildred Kitchen.

**Front Row among others:** Audrey Snowball, Rosemary Braithwaite, Margaret Mason, Edith Pumford, Miss Wilson, Miss Hedley, Laura Dixon, Beryl Walton, Winnie Cook and Marion Kipling.

**NORTH ROAD GIRLS CLASS 3**

**Back Row:** Jean Pennick, Ella Hall and Joyce Connor.
**Middle Row among others:** Audrey Cornish, Eva Cornish, Maureen Layton, Rosemary Ellis, Lily Raisbeck, Margaret Summerson and June Marshall
**Front Row among others:** Anne Stonely, Margaret Beavis, Marion Foster, Annie Jackson, Emma Howells, Annie Ward and Rose Ward.

**NORTH ROAD GIRLS MISS FISHBURNS CLASS**

**Back Row:** Margaret Spence, Barbara Button, Sheila Howe, Diane Ellis, Valerie Button and Ann Parkin.
**Middle Row:** Iris Lindsay, Doreen Vaudin, Bella Freeman, Rosemary Cummins, Margaret Bell, Dorothy Bulmer, Anne Simpson, Anita White, Maureen Welsh, Jean Campbell, Gladys Heathcoate and Iris Wilson.
**Front Row:** Kathleen Armin, Margaret Lisgo, Lily Birchall, Margaret Marley, Mary Wheatley, Miss Fishburn, Isabel Green, Olive Williams, Ann Brown, Jenny Hutchinson and Lillian Robson.

**NORTH ROAD BOYS THE SCHOOL GARDEN**

**NORTH ROAD BOYS SCHOOL MR. FOSTER'S CLASS c. 1951**

**Back Row among others:** Bob Blackett, George Jenkins, Cliff Patchett and Bob Cook.

**Middle Row:** Derek Davison, Jim Griffiths, Keith Greenwell, Harry Cartlidge, Barry Easter, Bill Yarrow, Ken Savage, Frank Snaith, Sid Constable, Sid Walton and Cec Preston.

**Front Row among others:** Tommy Wilson, Alan Laylor, Ken Smallman, Eddy Melonby Mr. Foster, Norman Taylor, Ralph Relph and Tommy Cook.

**NORTH ROAD BOYS SCHOOL MR.RODHAM'S CLASS c.1951**
**Back Row:** John Nathan, Billy Minto and Tommy Horniman
**Middle:** Cecil. Wheatley, Tommy Ellis, Peter Bowman, Bob Geldart, George Savage, Teddy Wager and Alan Sokell
**Front Row:** Billy Corbet, Billy Kipling, Eric Grayson, Dennis Curry, Ronny Evans, Mr. Rodham, Brian Miller, Wilf Brown, Norman Bulmer, George Richardson and George Armin.

**NORTH ROAD BOYS SCHOOL WOODWORK CLASS**

**NORTH ROAD BOYS MR. MILLERS CLASS c. 1951**
**Back Row:** Frank Wilkinson and Malcolm Rhodes.
**Middle Row among others:** Chris Dawson, Dick Taylor, Keith Lowes, Arnold Airey,
Ernie Hodgson and Bill Corbett.
**Front Row: Wilf Cooper,** Wilf Cooper, Glyn Taylor, Jim Bamforth, Bob Hoggard, Mr.
Miller, Eric Rounsley, Jim Temperley, Reg Pringle and Lance Bell

**SPENNYMOOR NURSERY NATIVITY 1963**
**Among others:** Marie Mulroy, Gillian Robinson, Gillian Blenkinsopp, Gail Berriman,
Angela Senior, Susan Birchall and Jacqueline Todd

# THREE

# TRADE AND INDUSTRY

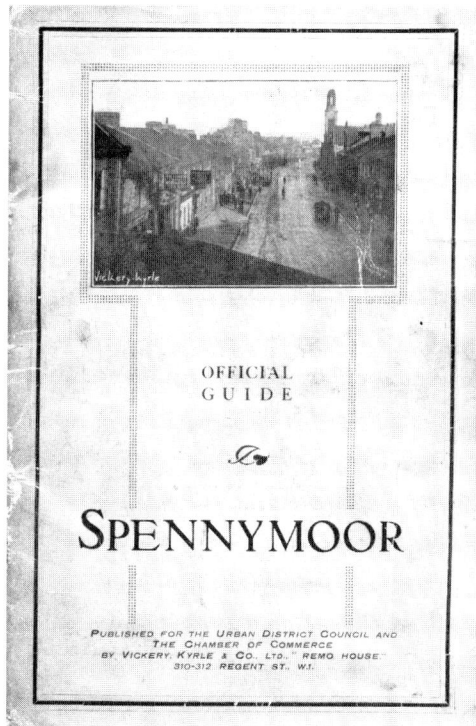

**TOWN GUIDE 1927**

In 1927, Spennymoor Urban District Council in cooperation with the Chamber of Trade produced an official town guide, perhaps the first that had been produced for the town? The guide gives a general picture of the town, at the time, along with a few facts and figures, photographs and descriptions of several businesses in the town. The following extracts and photographs have been selected from the guide to give an idea of what the town was like in 1927.

"Spennymoor is an important market town whose prosperity to-day is, to a great extent, governed by the fluctuations of the coal industry, situated some five miles west of Bishop Auckland, six miles from Durham and about 249 miles north of London. Communications between the town and the metropolis is established by means of an excellent service of main line trains running through Ferryhill Junction on the London and North eastern line to Scotland, and this junction also facilitates the attainment of other industrial centres in the northern area. Comfortable buses operate over a wide network of roadways in this vicinity, and effectually link up the town with such places as Bishop Auckland, Shildon, Crook, Stockton-on-Tees, Durham, Darlington, Barnard Castle, Middlesbrough, Hartlepool, Redcar, Saltburn, Newcastle and the intervening villages and hamlets."

At this time Spennymoor was the largest Urban district Council in the County of Durham.

"The town is governed by the Urban District Council of 21 members, and comprises the parishes of Tudhoe, Low Spennymoor, Whitworth and Merrington Lane. It also contains the ecclesiastical parishes of Holy Innocents of Tudhoe, St. Andrew's of Tudhoe Grange., St. Paul's of Spennymoor and part of Whitworth. In 1894, parts of the civil parishes of Ferryhill, Merrington, Tudhoe and Whitworth were added to the Urban District.

Spennymoor is now a Parliamentary Division and embraces Crook Urban District, Willington Urban District, Brandon and Byshottles Urban District and Tow Law Urban District."

"The town contains about 19,000 people, housed in 3,606 houses, and covers an area approximately 3,389 acres..

The Town Hall – in which are located the offices of the Urban District Council – Is a fine building, with a large adjoining Market Hall and also contains a large Assembly Hall, used for concerts, theatrical performances, etc., with a seating capacity of 750."

**TOWN HALL ASSEMBLY HALL**

"The Town Clerk is Mr. W. Robinson; the Sanitary Inspector, Mr. R. Bayles; the Medical Officer of Health, Dr. S.V. Tinsley; and Surveyor, Mr.C.R.Spencer."

"Spennymoor has, within recent years, rapidly increased in size and importance, this being chiefly due to the central position it occupies in a wide coal producing district, and in a remarkably short space of time it has grown from a little-known town into a place of considerable importance."

"A great improvement has been made by the reconstruction of the main road through the town. This is one of the main trunk roads from the North of Durham to Barnard Castle and the Yorkshire Roads, and now ranks as a first class highway."

While the main road was being reconstructed above the railway bridge the traffic was diverted up Craddock Street, which in effect became the main road through the town. The late Vince Robson, who lived in Craddock Street as a boy during the 1920's, often recalled that he and his pals used to climb the lamp posts in Craddock Street to catch pennies and halfpennies in their caps thrown by passengers in  charabancs that passed down Craddock Street on their way home from Blackpool.

"The town is mainly illuminated by gas supplied by the Tudhoe and Spennymoor gas Company whose works and offices are in Thomas Street. This is of good quality, and an adequate pressure is maintained both day and night. The Secretary and Manager of the Company is Mr.W.A.Cowley. The Company's showrooms are situated in High Street, and here a large selection of gas stoves and appliances for heating and lighting may be inspected.

The Northern Counties Electricity Supply Co., Ltd., have a power station in the town and supply current for private and commercial purposes

The water of the town – supplied by the Durham County Water Board – is both pure and abundant; the drainage system is modern and embodies, at the Council's works at Tudhoe, all the latest methods for the treatment and disposal of the efflux.

The Urban District Isolation Hospital, in Merrington Lane Parish, was built in 1902 at a cost of £6,500, and will accommodate 24 patients. (Hospital Lane opposite Rock Road Cemetery)"

## PLACES OF WORSHIP

Primitive Methodist Church, Rosa Street.
Wesleyan Church, Bishops Close Row.
Holy Innocents' Church, Mount Pleasant.
Presbyterian Church, Mount Pleasant.
St. Andrew's Church, Works Road.
St. Paul's Church, Whitworth Terrace.
Roman Catholic Church, Tudhoe Village.
St. David's Church, Tudhoe Lane.
Wesleyan Church, Tudhoe Colliery
Primitive Methodist Church, Tudhoe Colliery.
Primitive Methodist Church, Half Moon Lane.
Wesleyan Church, Mount Pleasant.
Baptist Church, Church Street, (Behind Town Hall)
Christian Lay Church, Church Street (Behind Town Hall)
Welsh Church, Clarence Street.

"St. Paul's Church dates back to 1858, when it was known as the "little church upon the hill," and it did not assume its present size and formation until later years. The parish Institute was inaugurated many years ago, as were also the Church schools – still known as Dyson's "Dicies" after the first headmaster – Mr. William Burkitt Dyson."

## SPORT IN SPENNYMOOR

### FOOTBALL

**SPENNYMOOR JUNIORS A.F.C. 1924-25**

" The Spennymoor Juniors A.F.C. had a very successful season in 1924-25, winning the S.W.Divisional Cup, the Bishop Auckland and District Medal Competition and being runners up in the Bishop Auckland and District Junior League and finalists in the Durham County Division Cup."
Hon. Secretary, Mr. Matt Wilkinson; Hon. Treasurer, Mr. B. Coia; President Councillor H. Askew; Chairman Mr. C. Pennington; Vice-Chairman, Mr. C. Hopper.

### CRICKET

"The Spennymoor Cricket Club's ground is situated at the west end of the town at Four Lane Ends. During its existence, the Club has won many distinctions, the latest being the Northern echo Challenge Cup. Many good players have learnt their cricket during their sojourn with the club, and are now assisting other organisations and playing in first class teams."

### GOLF

"The Whitworth Park nine-hole Golf Course is situated at Burton Beck, about one-and-a-half miles from the town. There is a comfortable Pavilion and the course is noted for its sporting nature, as also are the members of the Club, who are at all times ready to extend a hearty welcome to new members and the occasional visitor. The Club was inaugurated in 1912, and the present Hon. Secretary is Mr.C.Dixon of the Bank of Liverpool and Martins, Ltd. Spennymoor."

## SPENNYMOOR HOMING SOCIETY

"The Society has a large membership, and its members are fortunate in the possession of some excellent records. In 1913 a bird the property of two members, Messrs. Vester and Scurr, flew from Rome to Spennymoor, a distance of 1,093 miles, a record for long distance flying in Great Britain."

## EARLY SPORTING EVENTS.

"Few places of its size can claim to have played a more important part in the sporting world than this well-known iron and mining centre.

In the old days, fives or handball were much played at the old Tudhoe Park Grounds – the scene of many a great championship tussle. At cricket, Spennymoor could boast of a famous team, which used to play on the site now occupied by the Jubilee Park.

Race Meetings were frequently held near Four Lane Ends, where the Cricket club now hold their matches, and several famous horses have competed here under Jockey Club rules. Stirling a derby winner once ran at the meeting.

Pigeon shooting was another sport in which Spennymoor once took the lead, entries for the various events coming from all parts of the country, and it is interesting to note that the draughts championship of the world used to be decided in Spennymoor .

The old Rugby Team was once one of the best in England. At Association, Spennymoor have done great things, and today they have a very creditable team, which eminently maintains the traditions of the past.

Cuddy racing was once a popular sport in this part of Durham, and recently many pitmen kept a "racing stud." For the information of our readers, we should explain that the "stud" consisted of donkeys – but as most of the animals were specially bred for racing purposes, it took a good pony to give them any start.

Dog Fanciers are well catered for by the Spennymoor and District Canine Club, and the "Miller Challenge Cup," presented by Mr. Charlie miller, is competed for annually. Mr. Alex Bertram is a fancier of great experience, and his advice and service are always at the service of those who may find their pets are indisposed or ailing."

The cost of the booklet was mainly borne by the traders whose adverts appeared in the booklet. All were members of the Local Chamber of Commerce which had been formed in 1919 and every effort, at this time, was being made to get all traders in the town to join. The main aims of the Chamber of trade were twofold:

1. To reduce bad debt.
2. To bring pressure on the railway companies and cartage contractors to reduce the cost of carriage.

"In unity is strength; and collectively the traders of a town incorporated in one Association are enabled to obtain many concessions and advantages denied the individual. These are reflected in the price of goods and commodities for sale, and so ultimately benefit the purchasing public."

The booklet was distributed free or for a small nominal cost by the various retailers who advertised in it. The Chamber of Trade main purpose in supporting this publication was to exhort local people to shop locally. Some things never change!

## WHY NOT SHOP AT HOME?

"It is greatly to the advantage of private residents to shop in their own district.

If local traders do not receive support of their own townsfolk, they cannot give efficient service, offer goods at competitive prices, or employ local labour. Empty shops or a scarcity of local employment ultimately means increased rates.

Your local trader as a rule offers you equal value and his prices compare very favourably with those charged in the larger towns. His object is to please you, and he makes a strong bid for your patronage, both on grounds of the public spirit that supports enterprise and because he feels confident in his ability to serve you well.

Why pay bus or tram fares in order to shop in the large town? You seldom get as good value as you do at home; have to carry parcels about with you, perhaps lose some of them, and when you arrive home, fagged out, and find some of your "bargains" are not what you want; it is too much trouble to take them back.

If you are in the habit of getting all your requirements from the larger towns, or "shopping by post," why not try first what your local trader can offer? In these days of quick transit and special lines, offered by the big wholesale warehouses to even the smaller buyers; the local shops in a small town often offer exceptional bargains. The writer has seen goods in Spennymoor shops offered at a lower price than in larger surrounding towns. It is easy to understand why this is possible; the local trader's overhead charges, especially rent, are nothing like so heavy, in proportion, as those which traders in a big city have to pay. If he is a keen buyer, he can purchase his stock on the same terms as the big store. A small percentage of profit pays the local trader, and you benefit."

"With the object of pointing out the facilities which exist at your door, some of the businesses in the town are shortly described from the point of view of the man or woman, who is looking out for value and good service."

**HALF MOON LANE. LOW SPENNYMOOR**

## Miller's

The chief drapers offer value that will bear comparison with what is offered in any other district. This is a big store that caters primarily for the ladies of the town. Extensive stocks of wearing apparel are displayed, and these are always modern in design and manufacture. Here also, is a department which specialises in wall papers and home furnishings.

Though Low Spennymoor is slightly off the Main Roads in the Town

PEOPLE STILL FIND THEIR WAY TO —

# MILLER'S

The Shop for a Wonderful Selection of Cheap Wallpapers, and all Classes of Draperies at Prices which will stand any test of comparison

IF AT SPENNYMOOR TOWN
AT THE PRICES YOU FROWN
TO LOW SPENNYMOOR GO
AND SOON WE WILL SHOW
THAT PRICES ARE LOW
At **MILLER'S**
THE SHOP OF RENOWN

Miller's of Low Spennymoor

**HIGH STREET**

### Lidster's

Eat More Fruit – but eat the best. Lidster's, High Street, is one of the smartest and best kept Fruit Stores in the town. The writer would emphasize that there is always a splendid variety of fruit and flowers arrayed in this shop, and can record from personal experience that the window makes the mouth water in anticipation.

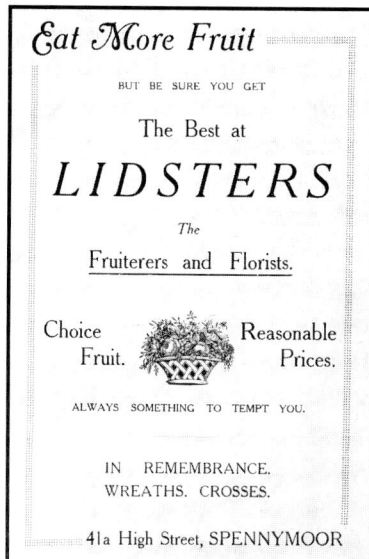

*Eat More Fruit*

BUT BE SURE YOU GET

The Best at

# LIDSTERS

*The*

Fruiterers and Florists.

Choice          Reasonable
Fruit.            Prices.

ALWAYS SOMETHING TO TEMPT YOU.

IN     REMEMBRANCE.
WREATHS.  CROSSES.

41a High Street, SPENNYMOOR

HIGH STREET
HARRISON'S AND DOBERMAN'S

G. Harrison,

Baker and           Established 1884.
    Confectioner.

When a business is well-known in a
town—when people make a point
of going to that one business for
certain requirements, it is a sure
sign that satisfaction is to be found
there. It is a sign that the proprietor
has the confidence of his customers.
It is a sign that the business is
GOOD.

Wedding
Orders,
Tea Orders,
Funeral Orders
attended to
promptly and
delivered by
our own Motor
Van.

This is the case with
HARRISON'S. Customers
recommend their friends to go there
because they can rely on the
QUALITY of the Bread and
Confectionery supplied.

Established
over
30 years in
Spennymoor

NUTRITIOUS BREAD.

APPETISING CAKES.

18 High Street,
SPENNYMOOR.

## G. Harrison Bakers, bakery in Cambridge Street, shop in High Street

One of the surprises of the town is the bakery of G. Harrison. Situated in Cambridge Street, and occupying the premises where the business was commenced 32 years ago. The outward aspect of the building does not give any indication of the inside equipment.

Once inside, however it is evident at a glance that the baking of bread and confectionery proceeds under well ordered, light, airy and clean conditions.

Ovens, machinery utensils, are of the most modern type, and there is a competent and enthusiastic staff, working under the direction of Mr. Harrison and his sons.

The firm are to be complemented upon their efforts to create the best possible conditions for the manufacture of their goods, and the town is to be congratulated upon having such care bestowed on the manufacture of its bread and confectionery as is given by this firm.

### S. Doberman, Complete House furnisher, High Street.

Another of Spennymoor's large shops is that of S. Doberman, Complete House Furnisher, High Street. A modern up to date shop, with excellent well lit showrooms. To the young couple about to furnish a home, or those who contemplate making alterations and additions to their house, this store will appeal. There is no need for the potential customer to disturb his capital in order to obtain all he wants for the "Home Beautiful," for Doberman's are pleased to supply him on the easiest of easy terms, and to rely upon every article being made of first class materials and workmanship. There is certainly no need to go out of town for furniture, while such a splendid selection and variety, at reasonable prices, are to be found at the door.

**DUNCOMBE STREET**

**W. Sample, Butcher, Duncombe Street.**

A really smart, clean and modern Butchering Establishment is in Duncombe Street, just off High Street. If one wishes for the best meat at lowest prices, it is safe to go to W. Sample. Quality and satisfaction are here.

PRIME BEEF, MUTTON
AND LAMB, AND PORK

HOME MADE SAUSAGES
(Fresh Daily)

You can't get better than THE BEST
and you get the best from

W. SAMPLE,

Family Butcher,

DUNCOMBE ST.,

SPENNYMOOR.

CHEAPSIDE

### B. Coia, Cheapside.

At B. Coia's Confectionery and refreshment Establishment in Cheapside, can be obtained delicious ice cream, and it's interesting to record that the proprietor obtained the Gold medal and Diploma for the best ices in the competition with makers from all parts of the world at the Centenary Exhibition held in Rome in June 1925. A large Billiard Saloon is also under the same proprietorship.

ICES

Which have been awarded the Gold Medal and Diploma
— Centenary Exhibition Rome June 1925 —

| The Ice Cream that is Guaranteed Pure | Made in a Hygienic Factory under Expert Supervision |

The secret is Pure Fresh Milk Cream Sugar and Eggs and
KNOWING HOW.

Quality the FIRST consideration.

| Wholesale and Retail Confectioner and Tobacconist | BILLIARD SALOON 4 Weardale Chambers |

B. COIA,
Successor to M Coia          Established 1887

5 Cheapside and 4 Weardale Chambers, SPENNYMOOR.

**HIGH STREET**

**W .Potts & Son, Sales by Auction, High Street.**

There are various ways of buying furniture for the home. If one's purse permits, the big furniture stores have always plenty of variety in new goods to offer – either for cash or on "easy" terms.

It is noticeable in Spennymoor that many bargains are to be picked up in the local Auction Rooms. Genuine sales of furniture and various effects are of frequent occurrence and prove a great boon to the young couple who are "getting a home together," and those who are refurnishing and adding to the home. The variety of goods offered is remarkable, and almost anything in reason may be obtained at some time or other. In these hard times, the sales must be a great boon to those of limited means.

# W. Potts & Son

AUCTIONEERS AND VALUERS

:: SPENNYMOOR ::

PERIODICAL SALES OF FURNITURE
and MISCELLANEOUS EFFECTS held
at our SALE ROOMS    Clients wishing their
Effects to be offered by Auction, should send
to the SALE ROOMS EARLY.

AUCTION  SALES  conducted  in  SPENNYMOOR  and
DISTRICT   A large following of buyers ensure good prices
being realized.

**HIGH STREET**

## Scott's

At Scott's the ladies will find the latest creations and fashions marked at prices that are specially tempting. Probably the ladies of Spennymoor already know that for value and style they cannot do better than Scott's

### Tudhoe Colliery Co-operative and Industrial Society Ltd.

A progressive and flourishing society, established in 1884 in the same small way these societies begin, it has rapidly attained its present size. The new premises in Tudhoe Grange were opened in 1919.

The Society is run on democratic lines, the members appointing their own Committee of Management, who direct the business policy of the Society.

The objects of the Society are to promote the social well being of its members by supplying the reliable goods at current prices, and at the end of each quarter the surplus over and above the expenses of management are distribution is divided among the members according to their purchases.

This is the fundamental principle which is a departure from the usual method of limited companies, who divide profits in proportion to the capital invested.

The members do receive interest on their Share Capital, however, in addition to the surplus divided, this being at the present time fixed at 5% quarterly. Thus the members are encouraged to put a little money by for the proverbial rainy day and at the same time earn a reasonable amount of interest.

Since 1923 the Collective Life Assurance Scheme has been instituted, by which all members are assured, the death benefits being calculated according to the purchases made. Large sums have been paid out under this scheme.

It would be true to say that the various operations of the Society enable it to be entitled to the term which was once applied by a well known statesman to the Co-operative movement, "a state within a state." The Society deals in practically every necessity of life and it would probably be safe to prophecy that within a few years the members will be able to obtain everything they need from their own stores.

The membership has grown rapidly and the sales reach a very big total each year.

**ATTWOOD TERRACE, TUDHOE COLLIERY.**
Showing Tudhoe Post Office and Tudhoe Co-op Premises.

**BEAUMONT TERRACE.**
**The Bishop Auckland Industrial Flour and Provision Society Ltd.**

The Bishop Auckland Industrial Flour and Provision Society Ltd., have Branch Premises in the town, situated in Beaumont Terrace. These were erected on the site of the old premises destroyed by fire on November 21st, 1922 and comprises the following departments:- Grocery and Provisions, Boot and Shoe, Ready-Mades and Tailoring, Drapery and Men's Mercery, Butchering and Milk.

Access to the first floor is gained by a main stair-way from the Drapery Department, and a second stairway from the Boot Department: the marble stairs are self supporting with and easy rise, and finished with mahogany newel posts, and Jacobean pattern balusters.

Adequate stockrooms are provided behind the respective departments on the ground floor, and an electrically driven lift is also provided between the various floors and cellars to facilitate the handling of goods.

Upstairs is the General Office and Strong room, also the Mantle and Millinery Departments, with work rooms at the west end.

The hardware, Wallpaper and crockery Departments with stock room, is at the east end, and the central portion of this floor is utilized as a Furniture Show room. The total dimensions of this room are 120 feet by 48 feet.

The whole building is lighted by electricity on the direct and semi-direct systems. Central heating on the low pressure system is fitted throughout.

At the rear of the premises is a commodious and up to date Slaughter house, Hunger house and Smalls factory, adjoined on one side by a fine range of stables, and on the other by Potato and Flour Warehouses. These rear buildings are separated from the main building by a large covered in yard. The Manager's and Horse keeper's houses adjoin the premises and the whole building occupies a site of one and a half acres, situated amidst healthy and desirable surroundings.

Motor buses pass the store at frequent intervals.

The Society's Central stores and Offices are at Newgate Street, Bishop Auckland.

**KING STREET**
Williams Wireless and Music Shop and G.W.Taylor's Tailor Shop

**The Wireless Stores, King Street.**

The Wireless Stores, in King Street, carry a big stock of everything necessary for the wireless enthusiast.

Gramophones and Records are in great profusion here and there is no need to dread the long winter evenings whilst one can buy entertainment at such reasonable prices as are offered at this shop.

WILLIAMS
*of*
KING STREET
SPENNYMOOR
FOR WIRELESS

Complete Installation and ALL ACCESSORIES. Local Depot
for BURNDEPT, MARCONI and POLAR STOCKIST.

**The World of Music and News**
brought to your Fireside

1, 2, 3, and 4-Valve Sets. Demonstrations and Advice Free

Gramophones—Columbia, Regal & Zonophone Records

*Williams, King St., Spennymoor*

HELLO !
YES  What is it ?
I've found a Good Tailor !
Who is it ?

G. W. TAYLOR,
2 KING STREET,
SPENNYMOOR.

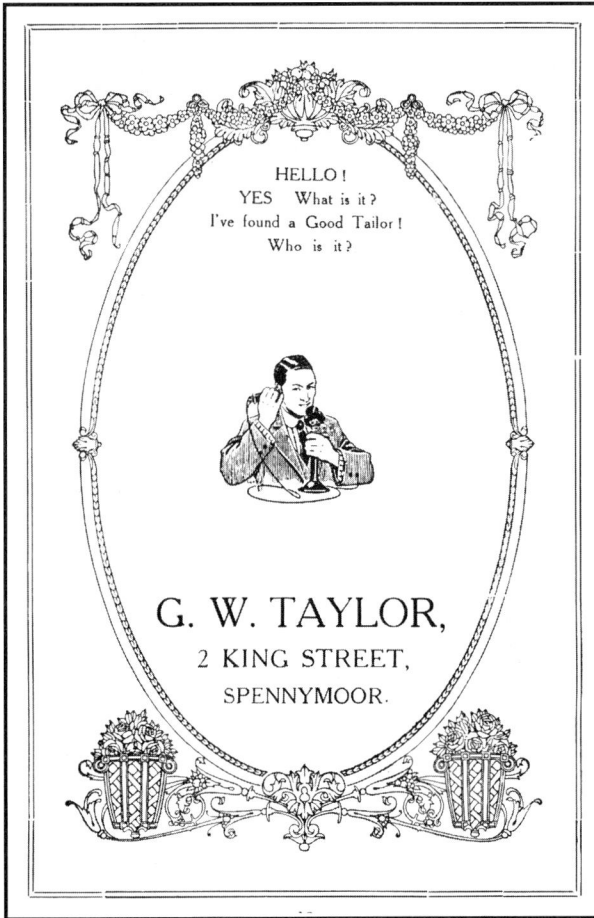

### G.W.Taylor, the Tailor, King Street.

One of the businesses that is undoubtedly up to date is that of G.W. Taylor, the Tailor in King Street. Here tailoring is evidently understood and a big trade done. Gentlemen's outfitting is another department of this business, and a glance at the windows will convince the prospective purchaser prices are lower than those ruling in most towns.

**BARNEY BUTCHER 1945**

J.W. Spencer "Barney" with his horse, "Butcher's Boy" in Todd Street. His butchers shop was in Whitworth Terrace.

**SPENNYMOOR CHAMBER OF TRADE OUTING TO RIPON 1924**

**THE VANS WHITWORTH c.1918**

**Back Row:** Anthony Barron, Pat Laidler, Dicky Showler, J. Thompson
**Middle Row:** R. Hughes, Elliot, Elliot, J. Dodds and Coleman
**Front:** G. Dibbs and W. Lindsay.

The "vans" were used on the Page Bank branch from Spennymoor to Page Bank Colliery. This branch line was very steep, running down towards the River Wear, it was opened in 1855. The line was 2 ½ miles long and a good length of that was at a gradient of 1 in 38. The gradient being so steep that locomotives were only allowed to haul five wagons of coal at a time. When the Bell Brothers took over the colliery in 1868 they rented it for £3 a day from the North Eastern Railway Company to transport their workers backwards and forwards to Spennymoor. Two vans were used and it is not certain whether they were hauled by locomotive or cable in the early days. By 1919 when the colliery was in full swing the number of men travelling per day had increased from about 90 to 250 and the rental charge was increased to £9 a day. At this time a locomotive was provided and the train consisted of three coaches and a brake van. The train went from Spennymoor to the sidings on the south side of the River Wear at Page Bank and then the colliery locomotive took the train across the river bridge to the colliery platform.

The first run was at 2.30a.m. for the 'foreshift', then back to Spennymoor and to Page Bank again at 5.30 a.m. for the day shift, then several times a day to suit the pit's shifts. The last run from page bank was at 4.30 taking home the "backshift". Special shopping trains were run on a Saturday so that the people of Page Bank could do their shopping in Spennymoor.

The colliery was closed in 1931 and the line was dismantled.
(The source of most this information is The North East Railway by Ken Hoole)

**THE VANS WHITWORTH**

Another group of pitmen waiting to travel down to Page Bank to the pit, unfortunately I have no names for any of them.

**MINERS CALL-UP EXEMPTION CERTIFICATE
FOR WORLD WAR 1**

**KENMIR'S FURNITURE FACTORY FIRE 1929**

Kenmir's were cabinet makers and had established their business in a small way in Spennymoor in 1897. Their first workshops were in the old Market Buildings in Silver Street on the site of what is now the Town Hall. Business began to expand quickly and they moved to larger premises in Charles Street in 1899. These premises are now used by Gordon Fletcher and Sons. By 1903 these premises had also become too small and a block of land was purchased to the north of Flora Street and a factory was erected on this site. Owing to continual expansion, additions were made in 1905, 1909 and 1914. The floor area of the premises was eventually expanded to about 40,000feet. And consisted of timber drying chambers, machine shop, cabinet and polishing departments, various stock rooms and a garage. The factory was equipped with modern English and American machinery, with all the shafting and belting underground. The firm produced furniture for the trade only and its chief market was the North of England. The average number of staff employed at that time was seventy.

The factory was destroyed by fire on the 6th September 1929 it was rebuilt on the same site and continued to produce furniture until 1964 when it was closed and put up for sale. The factory was vandalised and set on fire again and eventually it was demolished to make way for private housing.

**ROYAL ORDNANCE FACTORY WORKERS c. 1944**

**Among others:** Eric Grant, Edna Robinson, Jenny Barbour, Margaret Laidlaw, Janet Hall, Doreen Ellis, Mabel Cam, Aileen Temple, Sonny Feldt, Tom Eastwood, Maude Swinburne, Faith Stevenson, Ada Ellis and Doreen Ross.

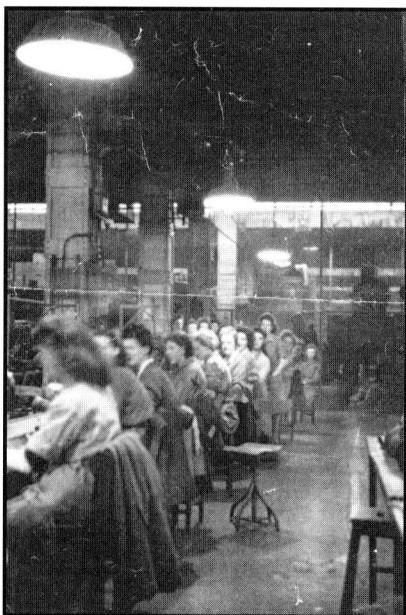

**ROYAL ORDNANCE FACTORY 1944**

Women and girls working on one of the munitions lines. The factory produced bullet and shell casings which were then sent on to the munitions factory at Aycliffe to be filled with explosives.

**DEAN AND CHAPTER COLLIERY
THE LAST SHIFT**

Miners from Spennymoor and Ferryhill arriving for the last shift before closure of Dean
and Chapter Colliery

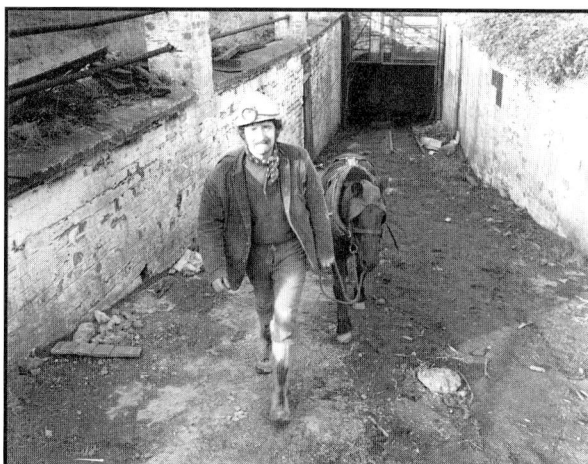

**JIM HENDERSON LEADING THE LAST PONY OUT OF
METAL BRIDGE DRIFT 1978**

**TODDHILLS STATION C.1930**

This station had originally been Byers Green Station on the West Durham Railway near where it made a junction with the Byers Green Branch of the Clarence Railway. Although there had been a station on this site from 1845 this station, called Byers Green although in Toddhills, was built in 1878. Byers Green Station was moved to its new site when the Burnhouse Junction to Bishop Auckland line opened in 1885. The engine shed can be seen in the left background, this engine shed was opened around 1878 to house engines that usually stood in the open at Spennymoor, the shed closed in 1922. These buildings were later incorporated into the brickyard and have only been demolished in recent years.

**UNITED BUS 1918**

United ran a bus service through the town from 1912. This bus a Daimler ran from Bishop Auckland via Ferryhill to Spennymoor and was driven by Mr. A. Burn. This was probably the first version of the Service 2.

WEARDALE IRON AND STEEL WORKS C.1900

TUDHOE COLLIERY c.1900 – BOILER STOKERS

PRICE ONE PENNY.

ORIGINAL LINES ON THE FATAL

# CATASTROPHE AT TUDHOE,

### NEAR DURHAM, APRIL 18, 1882.

## WRITTEN BY ALBERT CRAIG.

Together with as correct a list as is possible, to ascertain of the poor fellows who perished through the Explosion.

| | AGED. | | AGED. | | AGED. |
|---|---|---|---|---|---|
| A. Coldwell | 41 | John Cherry | 46 | Jas. Rhymer | 38 |
| Robt. Cairns | 21 | Thos. Jefferson | 61 | T. Shaw | 50 |
| W. Thomas | 46 | Jas. Whitter | 55 | Thos. Cook | 58 |
| W. Lambton | 22 | Jas. Cairns | 55 | Edw. Jones | 19 |
| Peter Strong | 61 | Thos. Armstrong | 16 | W. White | 56 |
| George Bowes | 50 | Hugh Armstrong | 19 | M. Cairns... | 24 |
| M. Butter | 59 | John Lambton | 16 | Henry Sloggett... | 16 |
| J. Gair, sen. | 57 | John Burns | 20 | J. Snowdon | 59 |
| W. Pinkney | 50 | George Stephens | 17 | Jos. Marsh | 59 |
| John Brown | 37 | J. Faulkner, sen. | 53 | Robt. Artus | 46 |
| Wm. Smith | 17 | Jos. Midgley | 62 | J. Patteson | 19 |
| Michael Rivers | 22 | W. Curry | 62 | Edmund Roberts | 17 |

Come brother drop a tear,
  Bow down thy head,
In silent grief draw near,
  Look on the dead.

Glance at each anxious face,
  Well may it seem,
To those about the place,
  Like some strange dream.

Hear ye the Orphan's cry,
  Of bitterest pain,
For loving hearts they sigh,
  But sigh in vain.

All future hopes are crush'd,
  Quick as a breath,
The merry song is hush'd,
  Silence'd by death.

I would I had been there
  The mother cried !
Dear ones would wish me near
  Before they died.

Have they no message left,
  No dying prayer,
Although of them bereft,
  I'll meet them there.

There were the lov'd ones meet,
  Those gone before,
Where we each other greet,
  And part no more.

No fearful accident,
  Can there annoy,
No trouble shall be sent,
  To mar our joy.

The cold damp grave receives,
  Their precious clay,
Their spirits dwell above,
  In endless day.

Weep, Tudhoe, weep, yea mourn,
  O'er heart's so true,
In the bright spirit land,
  They wait for you.

With Christ as our support,
  And sure defence,
We all may be secure,
  When we go hence,

Prepare to meet thy God,
  O Solemn Text,
The summons comes to all,
  We may be next.

*The Writer warns persons against infringing on the rights of these Verses as they are protected.*

**POEM COMEMERATING THE MINERS WHO DIED IN
THE TUDHOE COLLIERY DISASTER OF 1882.**

The disaster which occurred on 18th April 1882 resulted in the deaths of 37 men and boys an event which left the whole community shattered.

Work had begun on sinking Tudhoe Colliery in 1864 when it was recognised from the start that there were problems with gas both of the fiery and after damp types. The fiery gas was explosive and the after damp suffocating. In 1867 a Mr. Elliot of Newcastle after inspecting the pit submitted the following report:

"I inspected the workings of your new winning at Tudhoe with a view to reporting on the best means of ventilating the same.

I find that the works already executed consist of two shafts 12 feet in diameter both sunk to the Brockwell Seam which is found at a depth of 88 fathoms (528 feet) from the surface and passing through the Harvey Seam at a depth of 68 fathoms (408 feet).

Both seams are of excellent quality and thickness, the Harvey being 4 feet and the Brockwell 3 feet 6 inches.

During the sinking three very strong Blowers of gas came off in the drift made into the Hutton Seam to obtain communication between the two shafts which are 50 yards apart.

These blowers continue to discharge a considerable quantity of gas which is collected and brought in a four inch pipe to the surface where it is allowed to burn continually.

In the winning places of both seams a certain amount of gas is discharged from the coal, but not more than usually met with in opening out new workings in such seams.

Though it can hardly be said that this is a very fiery mine I am of the opinion that the indications are such as to require more than ordinary caution in arranging the means of ventilation and as the depth is moderate I would at once suggest that Mechanical ventilation will be the most efficient and decidedly the most economical that can be adopted.

To carry out this system it is to some extent necessary that the shaft used for the upcast should be ducted entirely for that purpose and as it is contemplated to draw coals out of both shafts there will be at first a little difficulty in carrying out this arrangement.

Looking at the large extent of the Royalty attached to this winning and the amount of work which is intended to be drawn out of the pits. I am of the opinion that the best and safest plan would be to sink a third shaft which could then be entirely devoted to the ventilation of the mine and I think this will be found to be the most economical in the end......."

By 1882 there were three shafts dedicated to the ventilation of the pit, two at Croxdale, an upcast and a downcast and another upcast at Tudhoe.

The explosion took place at approximately 1.30 a.m., there was a slight booming noise and the ground shook. Most of the men who were killed by burning and the violence of the explosion were in the main way those that were killed in the workings were killed by after damp. One of the rescuers was also killed by the effects of after damp. There were several theories as to why the explosion occurred, the one agreed as the cause at the inquiry was that a pocket of gas freed by a fall of stone had been ignited by a man travelling on a set of coaltubs with a naked light. Another theory was that gas had been ignited by a shot being fired and another that the shot being fired ignited the thin layer of coal dust which covered the walls and pit props. The latter theory was largely discounted as impossible at the time, but later explosions in other pits and scientific evidence proved that it might have been the case.

A full account of the disaster is given in The History of Spennymoor by J.J.Dodd.

**BRINGING OUT THE BODIES AT TUDHOE COLLIERY**

This is a well known photograph depicting the tragic event. The shaft on the left is the East Pit and the one on the right the West Pit. These were the original shafts sunk at Tudhoe. This scene is viewed from the north.

**TUDHOE COLLIERY c. 1910**

This is a view of the colliery from the south. The coals were led from the colliery by locomotive to the Tudhoe Iron Works via tunnel which passed underneath the Five-Lane- Ends. Some of the coal was used to produce gas at the Tudhoe Grange Gasworks at the top end of Barnfield Road, the rest either went to produce coke at the ovens on the Iron Works Site or was sent down to Hartlepool for export

THE

## PIT LADDIE INN

SPENNYMOOR

Prop.—Mr & Mrs J. C. Raine

### ALES

| Draught Beer | | Pint | 1/7 |
|---|---|---|---|
| Double Maxim | | ,, | 2/3 |
| ,, ,, | | ½ | 1/3 |
| Sweet Stout | | ½ | 1/3 |
| Export | | ¼ | 1/5 |
| Light Ale | | Pint | 1/7 |
| ,, ,, | | ½ | 10d |
| Strong Ale | | | 1/3 |
| Blue Label Bass | | | 1/6 |
| Lager Skol | 1/7 | with Lime | 1/8 |
| Guiness | | | 1/6 |
| Ginger Ale | | | 8d |
| Bitter Lemon | | | 8d |
| Tonic Water | | | 8d |

### NON-ALCOHOLIC DRINKS

| PUSSYFOOT | Orange Lime Blackcurrant Lemonade Grenadine Ice | 1/6 |
|---|---|---|

### SPIRITS

| Rum | | 2/6 |
|---|---|---|
| Gin | | 2/6 |
| Whisky | Prop Brands | 2/6 |
| Whisky | Extra Special | 2/8 |
| Brandy | | 3/- |
| Vodka | | 2/8 |

### LIQUEURS

| Advocaat | 2/4 |
|---|---|
| Dubonnet | 2/6 |
| Martini | 2/6 |
| Benedictine | 3/3 |
| Cointreau | 3/3 |
| Drambuie | 3/3 |
| Curacao Orange | 3/3 |
| Tia Maria | 3/3 |
| Cherry Brandy | 3/3 |
| Peach Brandy | 3/3 |
| Apricot Brandy | 3/3 |

### WINES

| Port & Sherry | 1/7 |
|---|---|
| Harveys Bristol Cream | 2/- |
| Baby Cham & Cherry "B" | 1/7 |
| All Fruit Juices | 1/3 |
| Cyder | 1/3 |

### COCKTAILS

| 1 | WHITE LADY. Cointreau, Gin, Lime | 3/3 |
|---|---|---|
| 2 | PERFECT LADY. Gin, Peach Brandy, Lime | 3/3 |
| 3 | PARADISE. Gin, Apricot Brandy, Orange | 3/3 |
| 4 | ROYAL LADY. Gin, Cointreau, Cherry Brandy | 3/9 |
| 5 | SIDE CAR. Brandy, Cointreau, Lemon | 3/9 |
| 6 | BLOODY MARY. Vodka, Tomato Juice | 3/9 |
| 7 | MOSCOW MULE. Vodka, Dry Ginger, Lime | 3/9 |
| 8 | CUBAN. Brandy, Apricot Brandy, Lime | 3/9 |
| 9 | T.N.T. Brandy, Curacao Orange, Orange | 3/9 |
| 10 | JAMES BOND. Vodka, Dry Martini | 3/9 |
| 11 | BETSY ROSS. Brandy, Curacao Orange, Port | 3/9 |
| 12 | ADMIRAL. Cherry Brandy, Gin, Lime | 3/9 |
| 13 | BETWEEN THE SHEETS. Rum, Brandy, Cointreau, Lime | 3/9 |
| 14 | CHOCOLATE SOLDIER. Gin, Dubonnet, Lime | 3/9 |
| 15 | MANHATTAN. Whisky, It Martini, Ang Bitters | 3/9 |
| 16 | HIGH HAT. Whisky, Cherry Brandy, Lime | 3/9 |
| 17 | KATINKA. Vodka, Apricot Brandy, Lime | 3/9 |
| 18 | BRONX. Gin, Sweet Vermouth, Dry Vermouth, Orange | 3/9 |
| 19 | PINEAPPLE BRONX. Gin, It. Vermouth, Pineapple | 3/9 |
| 20 | CZARINA. Vodka, Dry Vermouth, Sweet Vermouth | 3/9 |
| 21 | FRISCO. Whisky, Benedictine, Lime | 3/9 |
| 22 | SNOWBALL. Advocaat, Lime, Lemonade | 2/7 |

## THE PIT LADDIE BUFFET BAR PRICE LIST 1960's

The Pit Laddie was one of the first pub's in Spennymoor to be "done up". Vaux Breweries decided to attract couples into its pubs by providing comfortable lounges with a modern setting. Joe and Pearl Raine were the most convivial of hosts and the Pit Laddie lounge bar became a great success.

## THE VARIETY CLUB

The Variety Club was opened on Sunday 9th September 1966 in the old Clarence Ballroom (Rink). The refurbishment of the premises took four months to complete. On the first night the doors had to be closed after 45 minutes after the hall had been filled to capacity by 900 people. 100's of disappointed members were left outside. In its heyday the club boasted over 10,000 members. The owner the club was John Maguire and the manager was Sid McGee.

The first turns to appear at the variety Club were, David Whitfield, The Tony Faulkener Trio, Dance Trends Incorporated, Marina Monroe and Johnny Bell. As well as the turns there were five games of Bingo and also gaming rooms for the customers. They could gamble at Roulette and Blackjack.

**COUNCILLOR BIILY HIRST PULLS THE FIRST PINT AT THE TOP HAT**
The owner Sid McCullough and the manager, David Thompson look on.

TOP HAT NIGHT CLUB,
57 High Street,
Spennymoor.
Tel. 3047.

OPENING
JULY 15th, 1966.

Full or Part-time Vacancies for :
MALE & FEMALE BAR STAFF
CHEF, FEMALE COOK, KITCHEN STAFF.
CASINO STAFF & CASHIERS.
TRAINEE MANAGERS.
CLOAK ROOM ATTENDANTS & DOORMEN.
MALE OR FEMALE CLERK & JUNIOR TYPIST.

## THE TOP HAT

The Top Hat was opened on 15th July 1966. The club was on two levels in premises that had once been the Co-operative store. The ground floor had a restaurant and a gaming room where customers could play blackjack and roulette. The upstairs housed the cabaret area. The gambling used to subsidise the entertainment and many of the big names in show business performed at the Top Hat in its early years. Once the Top Hat lost its gambling licence the big name acts dried up and it went into decline.

# FOUR

# PEOPLE AND EVENTS

**Whitworth Park Banner.**

The banner was unfurled by Charles F. Grey M.P. for Durham and dedicated in St. Peter's Church at Byers Green by the Rector Arthur Leonard Russen on 22nd of July 1949.

The banner had been designed by the local lodge delegate Tommy Moult and made by the firm of George Tutill in London. This is the reverse side of the banner showing the Miners' Memorial in Durham Cathedral.

**Back Row:** James Willie Wigham, Fred Thompson, Joe Sheldon, Jack Chaytor, Artie Sellars, Bob Davison, Bob Cummins, Jack Coates, George Davison, Tommy Dargue and Alf Elwell.

**Front Row:** Tommy Moult, Arthur Russen (vicar), Charles Grey (MP Durham), Jack Robson, Gilbert Shaw, Sam Watson (Secretary Durham N.U.M.), Harry Raine, Joe Thompson, Nelson Morgan and Matt Simpson.

**Front of Whitworth Park Banner**

The front of the banner depicts a miner holding the badge of the Labour Party with the inscription "Let us face the future."

**Families of Whitworth Park Miner's who attended the ceremony at Byers Green**

**Whitworth Park banner being marched onto the field at Durham Big Meeting.**

**A later Whitworth Park Banner being marched past the balcony party at the Royal County Hotel**

The reverse of the banner shows Durham cathedral and Palace Green. The front showed a portrait of A.J.Cook, one time secretary of The Miners Federation of Great Britain.

**Tudhoe Mill Drift Banner 1958.**
**In King Street prior to going to the Big Meeting.**
**Among others: '** Dollar' Kelly, Terry Cook, Wilf Gill, Jack Hood and Alan Cook

**Dean and Chapter Banner c.1947**
Marching through Tudhoe Colliery on the way to the Miners Gala in Durham The
march started from the Vulcan pub in Low Spennymoor and carried on to Croxdale
where they all got on buses to take them to Durham.

**SUNDAY SCHOOL PRIZE GIVING AT THE ZION CHAPEL 1958.**
**Among others:** Maureen, Norma and Shirley Wintersgill, Doreen and Mary Boyes, Mary and Pat Morgan, Dora Tomlinson, Shirley Jaques, Brenda Simpson, Hilda, John, Terry and Billy Scott. Norma and Colin Turner, Pastor Williamson, Gilbert and Mrs. Anderson, Bill and Joyce Healey, Mary Bird and Bill and Dot Wilkinson.

**MERRINGTON LANE BOYS IN THE DAISY FIELD c. 1930.**
**Among others:** Jacky and Bobby Johnson, Ernie Curle and John Foster.

**MERRINGTON LANE CHILDREN c.1930.**

**Among others:** The Elliot Girls, Ruth Barras, The Wheeler Girls, Fred Fairless, Kitty Collingbridge, Lilly Barras and Teddy Curle.

**VENERABLE BEDE CHOIR, MERRINGTON LANE**

**Left side, front to back:** Teddy Hindmarch, Eric Crawford, Billy Foster, Harold Courtley, Tommy Griffin, Jim Loftus and Harry Hindmarch.

**Right side, front to back:** Teddy Courtley, Harry Courtley, Don Edwards, Dougie Wheatley, Ken Loftus and Jackie Fryatt

**THE NORTHCOATE BROTHERS MERRINGTON LANE.**
**1914 – 18 War.**

L to R; Andrew was blinded in the war, Bill was killed in action and Jack was badly frostbitten.

**OUTSIDE THE HEARTS OF OAK MERRINGTON LANE.**

The occasion being the 21st Birthday of Joyce Johnson in May 1952.

Vera Drake, Frank Overend, Freda Nicholson, Mabel Robinson, Peggy Hardy, Ray Barker, Hazel Robinson, Joyce Johnson, Jessie Curle, Margaret Curle, Nellie Downs, Nellie Angus, Alma Bray, Jean Brakewell and Becky Angus.

**MERRINGTON LANE
STALWARTS**

**From Back, L to R.**
Norman O'Hara, Teddy Curle, Bobby Blackett,
George Thompson and Eddie Jackson.

**THE HOSIE FAMILY c.1914**

David Hosie came from Scotland; he had been a farmer who had raspberry plantations.
He married Mary Hardy and lived in Merrington Lane and worked as a keeker (foreman)
at Tudhoe Iron Works.

The family are: Alec, Jack, David, Mary, Jessie, Edith, Janet, Hilda, Margaret, David
(junior) and Mary (the youngest).

**BLACKPOOL TRIP 1958**

**Among others staying at 62 Charnley Road:** Jack Hood, George Tolley, Sandra Myers, Fred Dunn, Betty Dunn, M. Marsden, Ally Dunn, Mrs. Tolley, Ned Hughes, Squit Hughes, Mrs. Hughes, Edward and Lily Marsden, Ian Dunn, Madge Hood, Edna Hughes, Jessie Grover, Dianne Orde, George Thompson and John Gardiner.

**THE BRIDGE INN TOURER C. 1958 AT 62 CHARNLEY ROAD, BLACKPOOL**

**From the back L to R:** Watty Boyes, John Scott, Fred Bell, Jake Angus, Joe Raine, Jack Cornish, Tom Hughes, Ken Curr, George Robson, George Warren and Cec Ship.

Eddy Bell, D. Smallman, Pinky Bradley, Jack Angus, Joe Angus, John White, Tom Purdham, Harry Griffiths, Jack Bell, Tom Kelly and F.Erwin.

Hopper Angus, G.Ryder, Harry Raine, Mat Angus, Toss Angus, Joe McCormick, Vince Robson, and G. Blair.

Steve Jaques, S. Bestford, Ernie Hughes, J. Hetherington, Jim Garret and H. Smallman.

**THORNS FACTORY ON FIRE**

**DEMOLITION OF HOLY INNOCENTS CHURCH.**

They are about to lift the steeple from the tower in the photograph. The story is that the steeple was bolted to the tower and the demolition people hadn't removed the bolts. After several attempts to lift the steeple there was much scratching of heads as to why it wouldn't move.

**GREEN LANE A.F.C. 1898**
Grandad Pinkney is marked by the dot in the front row.
This team played in Coulson's Field where the Sedgefield Borough District Offices are now.

**TUDHOE VICTORY CLUB TOURER c.1945**
**Among others:**
**Back Row:** P.McNulty, J.Tyler, J. Walker, P.Bott, J.Wilkes, M. Perry and J. Carr.
**Middle Row:** E.Carling, W. Hodgson, H. Guthrie, ? Hodgson, T. Smallman and I. Hindmarch.
**Front Row:** E. Stoker, Arthur Wregglesworth, J. Welson, T. Aspey, F. Smith and E. Hodgson.

**TUDHOE YOUTH CLUB HELPERS c. 1957**

**Among others:** Connie Waugh, Joyce Harker, Margery Snowball, Margaret Spence, Sheila Hodgson, Mrs. Fishburn and Maud Carling.

**TUDHOE VICTORY CLUB TOURER 1920'S**

**Among others:** J.R.Scurr, Bob Warren, Alf Kay, George Warren, Tom Middleton, Abe Hodgson, Jacky Peart, Jacky Hodgson, Bob Shevills, W. Swainston, Frank Edwards, Jim White, Bob Procter, Jack Hanratty, Will Chisman, Jack Myers, Billy White, Bob Overend, Jack Rowcroft, Jack Robison, George Wistill, John Ryder, Joe Ryder, Fred Hood, Jim Warren, Arthur Wregglesworth and Billy Wilkinson.

**TUDHOE METHODIST PICNIC 1920**

**TUDHOE METHODIST YOUTH CLUB 1951**

**Back Row:** J. Wilkinson, R. Bevan, B. Rowcroft, N. Harker, R. Taylor, J. Richardson, M. Penman, E. Spence, A. Elliot, J. Spence, B. Swainston, J. Dunn, D. Freeman and J. Pickford.

**Front Row:** O. Dobson, M. Dodsworth, B. Simpson, M. Spence, L. Nichol, A. Kirkup, N. Spence, M. Claughan, S. Willis, W. Rhymer, G. Waugh, P. Walton, Mrs. Graham, C. Waugh, H. Spence and V. Pickford.

**TUDHOE CRICKET TEAM 1950'S**

**Standing:** George Chipchase, W. Fletcher, J. Smith, D. Foster, Ray Fairly, Ray Scurr and T. Lumley. **Front Row:** Scorer not known, Peter Wilkes, W. Wilkinson, and Steve Adams, Jack Richardson, Jacky lane and Bob Burton.

**TUDHOE UNITED ASSOCIATION FOOTBALL TEAM 1904 – 05**
**Winners of the Croxdale and District League and winners of the**
**Richardson Challenge Cup**

**Back row:** R. Taylor (Hon. Treasurer), R. Lowes, H. Stitt, E. Edwards and J. Nelson.
**Third Row:** W. Hodgson, W. Lancaster (Trainer), J. Lowes, T. Potts, Wm. Cook, J. Nelson and R. McDonald.
**Second Row:** J. Haley, F. Eddy, W. Soulsby, J. Charlton, W. Brown and J. Pattison.
**Front Row:** J. Moody, G. Fishburn, J. Clarehugh, J. Cockayne (Captain), J. Rhymer and R. Dixon (Hon. Secretary).

**MAYPOLE DANCERS TUDHOE COLLIERY
OUTSIDE THE GOOD TEMPLAR'S HALL**

**TUDHOE COLLIERY FOOTBALL TEAM c.1902**

**Back Row:** J. Jefferson (Linesman), J. Scurr, H. Smart, T. Bussey, T. Elsdon, J. Johnson and R. Overend (Trainer)

**Second Row:** J. Lowes (Captain), J. Latheron, J. Hodgson, E. O'Neil and R. Dixon (Hon. Secretary).

**Front:** J. Clarehugh and J. Mitchell.

**TUDHOE COLLIERY FOOTBALL TEAM OUTSIDE THE COLLIERY INN.
WINNERS OF THE QUEENS HEAD CUP. C 1900**

**Back Row:** R. Taylor, A. Chisman, G. Shead, T. Eddy, W. Troup, W. White, R. Gray, S. Bunce and J. Fletcher. **Third Row:** R. Lowes, W. Godfrey, J. Towers, H. Patchet, F. Eddy, J. Scurr, J. Soulsby, W. Cartman and T. Hutchinson. **Second Row:** R. Overend (Trainer) R. Dixon, O. Gray, J. White, J. Lowes (Captain), H. Smart, T. Lowery, M.Troupe (Hon. Secretary), R. Soulsby, R. Troupe and (Trainer) **Front:** G. Blenkiron and G. Brown

**JACKSON STREET GROUP 1910.**

This was a street party celebrating the coronation of King George V, most of the participants being in fancy dress.

**TOURING GROUP OUTSIDE THE QUEEN'S HEAD IN VILLIERS STREET c.1910**

All dressed up in their Sunday best complete with buttonholes and no doubt raring to go, I wonder where too?

**BRIDGE INN TOURER to Blackpool 1960's**

**Among others:** Ian Hutchinson, Ivan Sewell, Kenny Appleby, Frank Kivel, Geoff Hutchinson, Peter McKiernan, Dave Cownan, Don Chapman, Billy Fryatt and Michael Grainger

**SALVIN'S TOURER c.1950**

Touring clubs were part and parcel of pub life at this time; the custom is still carried on today but not to the same extent that it was 50 years ago. The traditional days for touring were Bank Holidays, Easter Monday or Whit Monday, and the usual destination was a race meeting.

**Tudhoe and Spennymoor Co-operative Society Limited**

CHEAPSIDE, SPENNYMOOR, CO. DURHAM

TELEPHONE : SPENNYMOOR 3317

9th September 1966

Goods supplied to the SALVIN ARMS LEEK SHOW

| Prize. | Description | £ | s | d |
|---|---|---|---|---|
| 1. | Sewing Machine | 26 | 12 | 4 |
| 2. | Combunation Wardrobe | 24 | 19 | 0 |
| 3. | Display Cabinet | 23 | 17 | 6 |
| 4. | Cocktail Cabinet | 21 | 4 | 6 |
| 5. | Record Player | 19 | 19 | 0 |
| 6. | China Cabinet & Wine Glasses | 19 | 0 | 0 |
| 7. | Radio | 18 | 2 | 6 |
| 8. | Blankets & Electric Blanket | 17 | 0 | 0 |
| 9. | Table & 4. Chairs | 16 | 6 | 9 |
| 10. | Kitchen Cabinet | 16 | 6 | 9 |
| 11. | Electric Fire & Electric Toaster | 16 | 2 | 11 |
| 12. | Rocking Chair & Pouffe | 16 | 1 | 0 |
| 13. | Electric Food Mixer | 15 | 19 | 2 |
| 14. | Continental Table, Carpet, Tea Set | 15 | 11 | 11 |
| 15. | Bedding Bale | 14 | 14 | 0 |
| 16. | Bedside Cabinet & Ottoman | 14 | 3 | 6 |
| 17. | Clock & Coffee Set | 13 | 10 | 1 |
| 18. | Dinner Set, Tea Set, Canteen of Cutlery | 13 | 6 | 5 |
| 19. | Potato Peeler, Pans, Electic Kettle | 13 | 4 | 1 |
| 20. | Vacuam Cleaner | 13 | 3 | 6 |
| 21. | Ironing Board, Electric Iron, Clothers Drier | 12 | 18 | 5 |
| 22. | Rug, Steps | 12 | 7 | 5 |
| 23. | Bath Cabinet  Scales, Linen Box | 11 | 18 | 1 |
| 24. | Bedding Bale | 11 | 0 | 2 |
| 25. | C/wick Bedspread & Blanket | 10 | 16 | 9 |
|  |  | 408 | 5 | 7 |
|  | less 15% discount  ..   ..   .. | 61 | 4 | 9 |
|  | Net Amount due   ..   ..   .. | £347 | 0 | 10 |

**SALVINS LEEK SHOW PRIZE LIST 1966**

**LOW SPENNYMOOR METHODIST YOUTH CLUB, TRAMPS SUPPER.**
**Among others:** George Hall, Joyce Parkin, Mary and P. Walton, E. Prest, O. Button, G. Howells, Sheila Wigham, E. Spork, G. Lamb, G. Bland, R. Heseltine, K. Hindmarch, F. Howells, A. Crook, M. Robinson, E. Jewitt, L. Robson and H. Summerson

**HALF MOON TOURER c.1965**
**Among others:** Freddy Simpson, Ernie Minto, Billy Minto, Bobby Spowart (sen.), Bobby Spowart (jun.), Ray Pirt, Gordon Minnis, Harry Williams, Bob Bates, Pop I'Anson, Jim Shippen, Billy Bowtell, John Bolton, Tom Ward, Margaret and Jack Ramage (landlord and landlady)

**TIVOLI CINEMA STAFF 1949**

**Among others:** Jim Sapsed, Norman Blood, Julie Thompson, Margaret Hopkins, Ethel, Alma, Whit Hughes, Mr. Davis, Jean Russell, Janie Foster, Frankie, Jackie and Valerie Foster.

**OPENING OF THE NEW SALVATION ARMY CITADEL, DUNDAS STREET 1928**

**SALVATION ARMY PLAY PRODUCED BY LES PIPER c.1956**
**Among others:** Ian Tolley, John Scott, Jimmy Cummins, John Robinson, Malcolm Marsden and Peter Machin

**SPENNYMOOR CITADEL ANNIVERSARY 1963**

**SPENNYMOOR CITADEL BAND IN HIGH GRANGE ROAD**

**SPENNYMOOR ROUND TABLE FOOTBALL TEAM 1970'S**
**Among others:** Mike Gowland, Bill Carr, Graham Marshall, Tony Blenkin, Louise Blenkin, Alan Roberts, Mike Stephenson and Trevor Southern

**JUNIOR ACCIDENT PREVENTION COUNCIL 1961**

**Among others;** Carl Fletcher, John Gardiner, Trevor Storey, John Million, Barbara Gardiner, Bobby Moody, Malcolm Marsden. Geoffrey Foggin and John Gibbons.
The Committee was made up of local pupils and met in the Town Hall council chamber.
Barbara Gardiner was chairwoman and Malcolm Marsden secretary

## CORONATION DAY 1953.

Weather-wise Coronation Day was a disaster it poured down for virtually the whole of the day and as a result it spoilt many a well-layed plan for many of the local street parties that had been organised. But people weren't going to be put off by the weather and in most cases indoor venues were quickly found to hold the parties.

We lived in Pearson Street in Half Moon Lane at the time; we spent the whole of the morning watching the coronation on the television. I can remember that we had a house full of people mainly children watching the ceremony. In the afternoon we had our make shift party, crowded into the Allotment Association Meeting hut at the top of the "Little Lane". What a great time we had in there crammed altogether and being duly presented with our metal money boxes cast in the shape of a crown. Happy days but unfortunately no one was on hand with a camera to record the event. However, this was not the case at all of the parties being held around the town.

**CORONATION PARTY IN ROSA STREET CHAPEL.**
**These are all children from the Rosa Street area.**

**Among others:** Gwenda Pearson, Judy Pearson, Greta Pearson, Sandra Wigham, Keith Wearmouth, Alfred Wearmouth, Christine Wearmouth, Stephen Wearmouth, Dorothy Wright, Rita Richardson, Anne Lawson, Glenda Winterburn, Barbara Richardson, Pat Rooney, Billy Wright, Brenda Richardson, Alan Johnson, Jimmy Suddes, George Smith, David Macintosh and Neil Adams

**CORONATION PARTY IN ROSA STREET CHAPEL**
**Parent Helpers**

**Back row:** Margaret Wright, Mrs. Milburn, Mrs. Stevenson, Mr. Macintosh, Mrs. Wigham and Mrs. Pearson.
**Front row:** Mrs. Wearmouth, Mrs. Wright and Mrs. Winterburn.

**CORONATION CELEBRATIONS IN HUME STREET 1953**

## HUME STREET PRESENTATION

Mrs. Florence Greaves presenting a silver cup to Mrs. W. Harper of 2 Hulme Street Low Spennymoor, for her daughter Elizabeth Harper to mark the occasion of her birth on Coronation Day. The cup was subscribed for by all the people in Hume Street, the collection was organised by Mrs. Robinson and Mrs. Oliver.

**CORONATION PARTY AT THE SALVIN ARMS**
All the children are from the Deneside area.
Some of the families represented are: the Waterhouses, Burgess, Hughes, Hogg, Hepple, Watson, Meek, Holloway, Noddles and Bell.

**SPENNYMOOR AUXILLIARY FIRE BRIGADE c.1960**
**Back row:** Ray Garbut, Fred Bell, Eric Stapleton, and Paddy Alton.
**Front row:** Ernie Jackson, Mr. Smith and B. McGarry.

**THREE GENERATIONS OF THE PARKER FAMILY
IN VILLIER STREET c. 1950**

**GIRL GUIDE AND BROWNIE c. 1930**
A wonderful photograph showing the uniform styles of that era.
The Girl Guide is Dorothy Davies the Brownie Winifred Davies, the Davies family lived
at 5 Reservoir Cottages at the time.

The 'Works Reservoir' was a place we were told to keep away from when we were children, but of course it was one of the first places we made for to play. Below are two photographs of members of the Davies family for whom the reservoir held no fears as they seem to be using it as their own private pool..

**MARY DAVIES c. 1928**

**AUDREY SHAND AND DOROTHY DAVIES c. 1928**

As yet I have no photographs of Reservoir Cottages or Works Cottages which were adjacent to the works site, one lives in hope! However, the two following photographs of people from this area have in the background buildings of the long demolished " works."

**Juliet (Belgium visitor), Lydia Turner (father had the Dicky Pit at Middlestone Moor) and Freda Thompson.**

**FREDA AND JULIA THOMPSON C. 1950**
The tar and benzene plant is in the background.

The Thompson's lived in Works Cottages. Julie remembers that during the war despite the "works" being regarded as a target for German bombing raids they didn't have an air-raid shelter. Jimmy Coia, who was the Air Raid Warden, told them that if there was an air raid all the families had to take shelter in Jackie Broomfield's field which was in front of their houses. When there was an air raid the coke ovens had to be damped down, they used sacking soaked in water, so that the flames wouldn't show the bombers the way to the target. Julie says that it was so hot that the men's wooden clogs used to catch fire in the intense heat.

**HOSPITAL LANE CIVIL DEFENSE CENTRE 1940'S**
**Left to Right:** Barbara Tinsley, Cathy Robinson, Dorothy Davies and Sally Coia

**CIVIL DEFENCE AMBULANCE 1944**
**Barbara Tinsley on the runner-board**

**ANTI GAS TRAINING CERTIFICATE**

**COLLECTING FOR A SPENNYMOOR SWIMMING POOL. 1970'S**

Forming a line of pennies on Spennymoor Parkwood Precinct. There were regular collections made toward a building a fund for a swimming pool in Spennymoor. A lot of people thought that a swimming pool should have been built before the Recreation Centre. The lady on the left is Mrs. Nelly Bostock and in the centre background is Bill Smith one of the stalwarts of the campaign.

**SPENNYMOOR POST LADIES JULY 1944.**

During the Second World War many jobs previously done by men were taken over by women.

**Left to right:** Mrs. Ryder, Mrs. E. Brace and Mrs. Lindsay. Mrs. Lindsey worked as a post girl in World War 1.

**SPENNYMOOR PRINCESS 1962**

Doreen Williams, originally from Broom Street, Half Moon Lane, won the competition in 1962 when she was 22 years of age. She went forward to the Grand final in London but was not successful. The dress bought from Madame Meredith's for £10 and was all hand embroidered. Doreen was working at Siemen's at the time. The prize is being presented by Dr. Brauer, Madame Meredith is slightly out of view behind Doreen and the man with the beard was the owner of My Fair Lady, the hairdressers in Coronation Buildings.

**ST. ANDREWS GARDEN PARTY 1930'S**
The photograph was taken in the vicarage gardens in North Road
**Among others:** Sybil Waters, Mildred Kremner, Dorothy Davies and C. White.

**SMART AND BROWN PARTY 1951**
**Among others:** Hilda Brown, Mrs. Carrick, Joan Walker, Mary Shaw, Bessie Howe,
Gladys Wheeler and Julie Thompson.

**VJ DAY CELEBRATION SEPTEMBER 1945**

This celebration was organised by Fred Culine (extreme left back row) at Queen Street Square. The children were local from the Queen Street and Catherine Street area. The Culines were show people and had spent the duration of the war with their side shows and Noah's Ark on queen Street Square.

**ANOTHER VJ DAY CELEBRATION.**

This time children from the Baff Street area of the town. The photograph was taken prior to the party held in the British Legion Hall at Back Cheapside.

**SPENNYMOOR ROLLER SKATING RINK c.1932**
**Among others:** Billy Richardson, Arty Heseltine, Robert Ellis and Caleb Bird.
It was from the roller skating activities that the 'Rink' got its name, it is better remembered as a dance hall these days.

**LICENSED VICTUALERS DANCE TOWN HALL 1956**
Irene Carr, Jack Carr, Tommy Thompson, Hetty Forest and Julia Thompson

## THE CHRYSANTHEMUM MARKET

On the 24th and 25th of August 1939 a bazaar was held in Durham to raise funds for an extension to Durham County Hospital. Many branches of Durham County Women's Institutes took part each of them contributing recipes and household hints to a booklet which was produced to coincide with the bazaar..

Here are the efforts of some of the Spennymoor area members.

### SCRIPTURE CAKE

| | |
|---|---|
| 3 ½ cups 1 Kings 4, 22 | 3 ½ cups Fine Flour |
| 1 ½ cups Judges 5, 25 | 1 ½ cups Butter |
| 2 cups Jeremiah 6, 20 | 2 cups Sugar |
| 2 cups 1 Samuel 30, 12 | 2 cups Raisins |
| 2 cups Naham 3, 12 | 2 cups Figs |
| 1 cup Numbers 17, 8 | 1 cup Almonds |
| 1 tablespoon 1 Samuel 14, 25 | 1 tablespoon Honey |
| Season to taste with 2 Chronicles 9, 9 | Spices |
| 6 of Jeremiah 17, 11 | 6 Eggs |
| A pinch of Leviticus 2, 13 | Pinch of Salt |
| 1 cup of Judges 4, 19 | 1 cup Milk |

Follow Solomon's prescription for a good boy
And you will have a good cake, Proverbs 23, 14  Beat well

Mrs. Hanselman, Spennymoor

### BEEF MOULD

| | |
|---|---|
| 12 ozs. Cold minced Beef | Soak the bread crumbs in the |
| 1 teaspoonful Tomato sauce | stock or gravy, then mix |
| 4 ozs. Bread Crumbs | altogether, adding lastly the |
| 4 ozs. cold mashed potato | twp beaten eggs, put all in a |
| 1 teaspoonful Vinegar | greased mould and steam for |
| ¼ pint Stock | an hour. |
| 2 Eggs, Salt and Pepper. | |

Mrs. R. Elwell, Page Bank

### AN INEXPENSIVE FURNITURE REVIVER

| | |
|---|---|
| 1 dessert spoonful Salad Oil. | Mix Well. Dip a piece of |
| 1 dessert spoonful Paraffin. | flannel in very lightly and |
| 1 dessert spoonful Vinegar. | rub over furniture well, an |
| | polish with a soft duster. |

Mrs. J. Lynn, Page Bank

### RECIPE FOR OLD PEOPLE'S COUGH

| | |
|---|---|
| 1 tablespoon Vinegar. | This makes a small quantity |
| 1 tablespoon Syrup (Treacle). | and can be doubled if needed. |
| 1tablespoon Colman's Mustard. | |

Mrs. George Ridley, Spennymoor

# FIVE

# PAGE BANK

**PAGE BANK WEST TERRACE 1935 AFTER THE RIVER WEAR HAD BURST IT'S BANKS.**

The River Wear was prone to flooding during the winter months the seriousness depending on the amount of rainfall.

Although Page Bank was always a separate community to Spennymoor the people were closely connected with the town. This was despite the fact the it was administered by Willington Urban council. People found employment in Spennymoor, they shopped there and they also found their entertainment there in the pubs and picture houses.

The origins of the name Page bank according to the latest research by Victor Watts in his excellent book, A Dictionary of County Durham Place Names, is as follows. The first mention of the place was in 1625 as Pedgbanck and then in 1856 as Page Bank the meaning being 'Hill belonging to the Pegge family.' There is however a local version of how the place got its name which is that bobby Shafto was courting a girl on a nearby estate and whenever he wanted to see his lady he sent a page down Whitworth bank to see if she was at home.

Up until 1853 Page Bank was strictly an agricultural area then came the sinking of the pit and the place developed into a community of over a 1000 people.

Below is given a written account describing the village around 1955 whether it is a personal account or the copy of a newspaper report I am not able to establish.

It is said that Page Bank the old mining village two miles from Spennymoor and a similar distance from Willington is a village without a future due in large a measure to its geographical situation and the fact that the majority of houses are old and weather beaten, with little or no prospect of being replaced.

At the same time there are people living in the village who would not like to leave because it has lost its pre-war days of depression when the majority of the population of 700 men women and children existed on the dole. Now the men are working and their families are much happier. Some are employed on the trading estate at Spennymoor, others are working at Whitworth and Brancepeth Collieries and a few a little further afield.

The streets, however, are still in bad condition but some of the houses although condemned are still occupied by villagers who like the happy carefree atmosphere of a friendly community.

Gone, however, is the colliery which for 80 years provided the village with its chief source of employment. Known as Page Bank Colliery, it was sunk in 1853 by the Attwood & Company. It later became the property of Ralph Ward Jackson of Hartlepool and then Bell Brothers of Middlesbrough took it over. In its 'dying' years it was owned by Messrs. Dorman Long and Company.

The Busty Seam approximately 5 foot thick produced thousands of tons of high class coal. The pit had a daily output of 850 tons, the number on the payroll at the time being in the region of 600. Most of the coal was converted into coke on the site there being at the time 312 coke ovens

There are a good number of old age pensioners in Page Bank the oldest being Mrs. Sarah Hamilton who is aged 87 and lives at 56 Long Row. She has lived in the village for nearly 50 years occupying the same house all that length of time. Living with her is her son Robert aged 47 who works outside the village. Mrs. Hamilton though feeble is still able to do her housework read the papers and attends the cinema shows in the social services hut. Mrs. Hamilton has smoked a pipe for 56 years. After Mrs. Hamilton comes 80 years old Thomas Heslop an old miner who wrought coal in the local pit for 50 years or more. He now takes part in all the social activities of the village. He is an expert leek grower one of many in the village. Over and above he is an authority on all phases of gardening and he spends his weekends 'waiting' on at the local. "I have lived here nearly all my life and if I were to begin life all over again I think I would live in Page Bank especially if the times were as good as when I was a boy."

**BOB HODGSON SENIOR AND JUNIOR WITH SHOW LEEKS**

24TH April 1959

The storeroom of Page bank community Centre burned down. The 60 foot long building was the headquarters of the local branch of the British legion and the Women's Institute. The Women's Institute piano was destroyed as was some sporting equipment and some furniture.

The Community Centre was completely burned down on Good Friday morning in 1965.

Page Bank School closed on 9th April 1965 and the building was bulldozed on the 14th April 1966

Bob Milburn's shop and 2 houses were bulldozed down in Railway Terrace on 30th April 1966.

111

**PAGE BANK YOUTHS 1921 (title on back of photograph)**
**Left to Right:** Robbie Waugh, Billy Simpson, Tommy Ellis, Bob Hodgson, Alfie Taylor and Jim Hodgson.

**PAGE BANK BRIDGE 1954**
The old wooden railway bridge was replaced and a new road with a footpath was laid. The road was only wide enough to take one-way traffic.

By 1961 the village school only had 37 infant and junior pupils the older children went to Willington Secondary modern school.

In 1961 Page bank was declared a Category D Village.

During the early to mid 1960's most of the residents worked in Spennymoor and there was a fear that young people would leave the village and further reduce the dwindling population. Page Bank was felt to have been left behind by the rest of the Spennymoor area. Most houses still had ash closets and the village was only a fraction of its previous size due to slum clearance. There was only one decent road and that was the main road between Spennymoor and Brancepeth all the others were glorified cart tracks which became a nightmare in winter.. Despite this most of the villagers were opposed to moving to new housing estates outside the area as most had been born and bred in Page Bank. There was very little in entertainment in the village apart from the Women's Institute and the local pub the Shafto Arms. There was at the time though a good bus service to Spennymoor. There were three shops in the village most women did their shopping there and could get most of what they required.

## Mrs. Lynn

At this time Mrs. Lynn aged 83 of 15 East Terrace was the oldest resident. She had come to the village from Willington 63 years before and had lived in the same house for over 50 years; it had previously belonged to her husband's parents. She was 21 years old when she married and moved to Page Bank.

"This was a lovely little mining village. You could eat your meat off anyone's doorstep, people were so proud of the place. All neighbours who were akin to each other through marriage worked hand in hand and all the houses had lovely gardens. Concert parties and dances were held regularly.

The school used to be the pride of the village with everyone attending."

Mrs. Lynn had 40 great grandchildren, 14 grandchildren and 5 children

## Mr. Cockburn.

Mr. Cockburn of 13 East terrace was 79 in 1961. He began work in the pit in 1894 when he was 12 years old for a shilling a day. In 1902 he followed in his fathers footsteps and became an overman and was made up to a mans wages.

"It used to be a pleasant prosperous place. We had two lovely churches here with some of the best singers in the county in the choirs. The Shafto Arms was built in 1900 and before that people used to drink in an off license up at Stanners Farm.

The pit gave each household in the village a load of manure from the pit ponies for the garden. If the gardens weren't kept tidy you were called in front of the pit manager. No one was allowed to keep a dog."

Wilkinson's buses started running through Page Bank to Willington on 16th May 1963 The Page Bank bus service ended on 6th September 1969

**BOB AND JIM HODGSON WITH SHOOTING TROPHIES 1933.**

Apparently there was a thriving rifle shooting club at Page Bank during the 1930's I would be glad to hear any information that anyone may have about it.

**FANCY DRESS AT PAGE BANK**

Probably from the early 1930's but unfortunately there are no names to go with the photograph.

### Anon

"I remember the village in its prime. I can see a little lad walking hand in hand with his Mam and Dad through the fields from Byers Green and crossing the river in a magical boat on a rope, a ferry that never touched water.

I remember a brass band playing in the sunshine' the neat rows of houses with their scoury stone whitened steps, the gay gardens and a remarkable absence of dogs. I have a theory that the latter was a relic of the days of the Pitman's Bond, which outlawed asses and donkeys to restrict independence and dogs so as to preserve the gentry's game.

If I was to build a monument it would be raised to a way of life and the heroes it produced – the men who risked death to rescue their comrades, the ranters who preached the good life in the tiny brick chapel, the miners who battled for their union and the women who sustained them."

**SARAH HODGSONS 21ST BIRTHDAY PARTY c. 1933**

### Water Shortage.

On 25th January 1963 the pipe which carried Page Banks water supply over the River wear froze solid and cut off the water supply to the village. The only source of water was the pub the Shafto arms which was on the Spennymoor side of the river. The village population of about 500 usually used about 12,000 gallons of water every day . The whole village had to be supplied from the pub and the villagers made the 300 yard trek with buckets, pans and bottles.

Men went to work unshaven, washing piled up and Harold Williams the landlord of the pub stated that he had never known water to be more popular than beer. He said he had seen blokes in here who swore blind they would never go into a pub. Kids came for water and they were trying to sell it for a penny a bucket.

The Water Board tried to thaw the pipe with flame throwers but the ice wouldn't give so they brought a water cart which held 3,000 gallons and replaced it as and when needed.

**PAGE BANK TOURER 1930'S**

**THE TERRIBLE STATE OF THE ROADS BETWEEN THE PAGE BANK ROWS**

**ST JOHNS AMBULANCE BRIGADE AT PAGE BANK CARNIVAL 1930's**

**PAGE BANK SCHOOL 1930**

The fate of Page Bank village was laid on the night of November 5th 1967.

Note in the scrap book of Mrs. Morgan for Nov. 5th

"A night of terror and disaster when flood waters 5 feet high hit our small village."

Flood water rushed into the houses reaching as high as 10feet in some. Civil Defence workers, Sea Scouts, Fire Brigade, W.V.R.S., Police and Ambulance services came to the aid of the devastated village. Lots of people had to be evacuated, at first many people were not keen to move to villages in the Crook and Willington areas, they preferred Spennymoor, but now they were willing to go anywhere.

In the March of 1968 Page Banks only pub closed. There were only 36 houses occupied in the village most of the others had been rehoused in the Willington area. The pub owned by Cameron's was at a low ebb and had not being doing very well even before the disaster of the flood.

In 1965 the pub had sold 127 barrels of beer
In 1966                   94
In 1967                   77

In the September of 1968 the last residents of Page Bank were set to sell their houses to the local council. The houses on New Row were without sewerage and proper access roads and Durham County Council recommended that Crook and Willington Council buy the houses and rehoused the people and make Page bank an agricultural village again.

Only 19 families remained most of them would have preferred to go to Spennymoor rather than Crook or Willington but they were worried about the danger of flooding again.

After a 115 years the community of Page Bank ceased to exist.

Most of the information for this chapter on Page Bank came from the wonderful scrap books that have been kept by Mrs.Morgan once a Page Bank resident but now living at Willington. Mrs. Morgan's husband Albert was killed at Whitworth Park Colliery on 23rd January 1957.

The photographs came from Mrs. Betty Waugh from Coxhoe who although not from Page Bank had relatives there. As well as these photographs I have a collection of 85 Page Bank photographs from another source. They are all photographs of people and seem to date from around the 1st World War making it difficult for any of them to be recognised. A clue is the name and address of Mr. T. Lawson 32 Railway Terrace, Page Bank on the back of one of the cards. If anyone would like to look at them an perhaps help to identify any of the people please don't hesitate to contact me.

# SIX

# EARLY DAYS

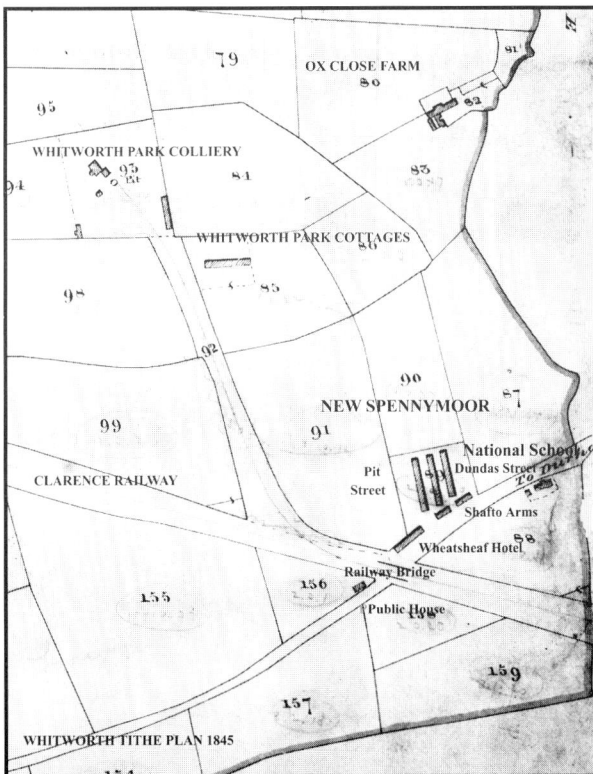

**NEW SPENNYMOOR**

One of the earliest representations of Spennymoor on a map. The section shown is taken from a Tithe Plan of 1845 deposited in Durham University Library.

Spennymoor was also referred to as New Whitworth at this time. Most of the land covered by the area of the map was owned by Robert Eden Duncombe Shafto who lived in Whitworth Hall with his family.

The earliest buildings were those associated with Whitworth Park Colliery, the earliest dwellings being Whitworth Park Cottages. (*If anyone one has a photograph of these cottages I would be most grateful for a copy*). These cottages were demolished around about 1947 or 1948 and the only photograph I have is the one below.

**Grandma Kelly outside No. 11 Whitworth Park Cottages c. 1935**
**The rest of the row can be seen stretching into the background**

Grandad Kelly was a tinsmith (tinker) by trade who made his tin goods on the premises. Number 11 was the biggest cottage in the row and must have been occupied by a colliery official at one time. Grandad also owned the paddock next to the cottage which is still in existence and still known as Kelly's Field.

The main centre of population, which numbered 290 in the 1841 census, was centred on three rows of pit cottages in the Dundas Street area; these apparently were known as Whitworth Rows. The rows of pit cottages were built quickly and cheaply and consequently they were what we might term "jerry built". Most of them had one or two rooms and a loft which was reached by a ladder. They were overcrowded as there were not sufficient houses to house individual families, sometimes it was one family to a room and almost every household took in a lodger. There was no running water and no sanitation so that the occupants lived in unbelievable squalor by today's standards. The water was piped from the colliery to a tap at the end of each row and all waste including human waste was deposited in a wooden ash box outside the front door. These were supposed to be emptied at regular intervals but never were. It's not difficult to imagine the smell that would arise from these in the warm weather. During wet weather the boxes used to overflow and turn into an evil stinking mess that people had to trudge through.

These cottages were soon demolished and replaced by larger but not necessarily better houses.

The main street at this time was virtually non existent; the only building on the south side of the street was the National School which had been built in 1841 by the Reverend Vicar of Whitworth. The building was of some architectural interest as it had been designed by Ignatius Bonhomie; sadly nothing remains of this building today nor seemingly any decent photographic record. On the north side of the street it is said that the first building was on the site of what is today the Station Guest House, it was a public house but the name of it has been lost over time. This was the first building in Spennymoor to be built "above the bridge" on the western side of the railway bridge. Next came the shops on both corners of Dundas Street and just down the street from them the Shafto Arms, a low building at this time which later had a brewery built out the back.. This building was replaced by one of the tallest buildings in Spennymoor and which is still standing on the corner of Oxford Road and houses a pizza shop and a clothes shop. Then came the Wheatsheaf Hotel which as well as being a public house was also the post office.

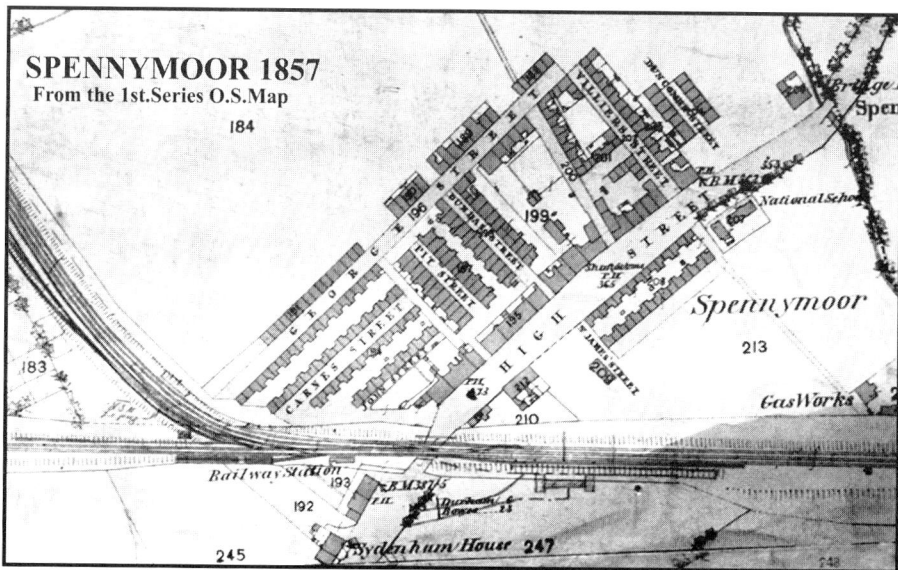

**SPENNYMOOR 1857.**

This is the picture 12 years on; Spennymoor now had a rapidly growing population due to the opening of the Iron Works in 1853. The north side of the main street is beginning to take shape and behind it the original Dundas street and Pit Street have been replaced with new houses and a good deal of new building has taken place. On the south side of the street two rows of miners cottages have been built, the ones fronting the main street were soon converted into shops and formed the basis for Spennymoor's covered market. The row of cottages behind was Silver Street which later housed the Local Health Board offices when the Local Health Board was established in 1863. This was the site that the present Town Hall buildings were constructed on in 1912. A gas works was also in existence and a railway station had been built to the west of the railway bridge.

## THE 1851 CENSUS

Between 1801 and the 1830's there had been a gradual decline in the population of Whitworth, probably a natural decline rather than people moving away However, by 1841, there was a dramatic increase in population of over 100% to 290. This can be attributed to the coming of the railway and exploitation of the Whitworth Coal Royalty. In the following decade there was a further dramatic increase this time by 200%, which was the direct result of increased activity at Whitworth Colliery.

By 1851 there were 112 occupied dwellings in Whitworth, these being occupied by 366 males and 293 females, making a total population of 659 persons. Thus in the space of little more than a decade Whitworth had grown from a small agricultural community into a pit village which was to continue developing into a sizeable town by the time the nineteenth century was out.

Who were these people who moved into Whitworth? Where did they come from and what were their occupations?

The counties of Northumberland and Durham were the two main counties of origin for most of the population of Whitworth. The people from these areas were mainly pitmen and their families who had come from other mining communities, within the two counties. The majority of them seemed to have been experienced miners, having worked in several collieries before coming to Whitworth.

There were two small contingents, within the population from Ireland and Wales. The welsh of course were miners, the Irish had probably been members of the navvy gangs involved in the construction of the Byers Green Branch Railway and had turned to mining or had reverted to their original occupations as farm workers. The sole representatives of Devon and Hereford would also have probably left work on the land to become navvies, and when the opportunity had arisen had reverted back to their original occupation on the land. There was a small contingent from Cornwall, in all probability ex tin miners. It was well known fact that where there was a mining community, of any kind, you would find a Cornishman.

The majority of Scots were involved in farming or domestic service; only one family being involved in pit work. The Scots seemed to be a close knit group within the community; the Scottish farmers employed mainly Scottish labour, the Scottish Land agent employed mainly Scottish servants; the pitman and his family took in Scottish lodgers.

Yorkshire provided a number of agricultural workers; however, there were several mining families among them.

Along with the mining community and the agricultural community were the occupants of Whitworth Hall and their staff of servants, there were also local craftsmen, traders and a few professional people.

## COUNTIES OF ORIGIN OF THE POPULATION OF WHITWORTH 1851

| COUNTY | MALES | FEMALES | TOTAL |
|---|---|---|---|
| Cheshire | 1 | | 1 |
| Cornwall | 3 | | 3 |
| Cumberland | 3 | 2 | 5 |
| Derbyshire | 5 | 2 | 7 |
| Devon | 1 | | 1 |
| Durham | 230 | 196 | 426 |
| Hampshire | 1 | | 1 |
| Hereford | 1 | | 1 |
| Lancashire | 3 | 2 | 5 |
| Leicester | | 1 | 1 |
| Northumberland | 67 | 54 | 121 |
| Nottingham | | 3 | 3 |
| Westmorland | 1 | | 1 |
| Yorkshire | 23 | 18 | 41 |
| Ireland | 8 | | 8 |
| Scotland | 18 | 12 | 30 |
| Wales | 3 | 1 | 4 |

Of the total population of 659, 203 were children; some of the families were large having as many as eight children. A good number of these children attended the National school. Most of the boys when they reached their early teen were employed in pit work. The youngest boys employed in Whitworth Pit in 1851 were two ten year olds.

Many of the households took in lodgers as there was a serious housing shortage and there were no special provisions for single men. In most cases one or two lodgers were taken in. most of the larger households had house servants, usually young girls between 14 and 28 years, who lived with families who employed their services. Most of the girls came from surrounding towns and villages and in some cases were relatives of the families they worked for. Some however were from as far away as Derbyshire and there is no indication to suggest that they were relatives. Thus some of the larger households, such as that of Edward Blewitt, miner, numbered up to as many as thirteen occupants:
Edward Blewitt, his wife, seven sons, one daughter, two lodgers and a house servant.
Some of the families in Whitworth had lived and worked in a variety of places before settling there, as the birth places of their children testify. This applies to agricultural community as well as the pitmen:

Edward Coulson, pitman born in Durham, met and married his wife while working in Northumberland. He returned to Durham, his first son being born at Houghton le Spring, his second at Easington; his first daughter at Shincliffe; his second at Merrington and his third at Seaham. Whitworth was the seventh place that he had lived and worked at up to 1851.

John Fletcher, bailiff, born in Yorkshire his first daughter was born at Sockburn: his first son at Heighingtron; his second daughter at Byers Green; his second son at Hetton and his third daughter at Byers Green. This indicates five moves before arriving at Whitworth. It could of course be that he had been a miner and changed his occupation to bailiff.

Only four families had been born at Whitworth and had spent most of their lives there. These were:-

John Hetherington, pitman and his family of wife, two daughters and five sons.
John Pattison, butcher, and his family of wife and two sons
James Adamson, joiner, wife (born at Lanchester) and his two daughters.
Thomas Dobby, colliery banksman, wife (born Bishop Auckland) and daughter and three sons.

There was very little in the way of employment for the older daughters of families, most seemed to remain at home and help to run the households. The six who were employed were either concerned with dressmaking or were agricultural labourers, the latter being the daughters of farmers.

## OCCUPATIONS OF THE PEOPLE OF WHITWORTH 1851

### EMPLOYED AT THE COLLIERY

| | |
|---|---|
| Pitmen | 168 |
| Pitboys | 14 |
| Colliery labourers | 17 |
| Colliery Viewer | 1 |
| Colliery Joiners | 2 |
| Colliery Banksmen | 4 |
| Colliery Blacksmiths | 2 |
| Colliery Overmen | 1 |
| Colliery Sinker | 1 |
| Colliery Mason | 1 |
| Colliery Brakeman | 1 |
| Colliery Furnaceman | 1 |
| Engine Wrights | 2 |
| Coke Burners | 2 |

### EMPLOYED ON THE RAILWAY

| | |
|---|---|
| Plate Layers | 1 |

# SPENNYMOOR REMEMBERED BOOK - 4

## EMPLOYED IN FARMING

| | |
|---|---|
| Farmers | 5 |
| Farm Labourers | 23 |
| Bailiff | 1 |
| Dairy Maids | 3 |
| Sawyers | 1 |
| Woodman | 1 |

## SERVANTS

| | | | |
|---|---|---|---|
| Parlour Maids | 2 | Governess | 1 |
| Lodge Keeper (female) | 1 | Nurse | 1 |
| House Keepers | 4 | House Servants | 17 |
| House Maids | 3 | Kitchen Maids | 1 |
| Cook | 1 | Grooms | 1 |
| Gardeners | 2 | Under Gardeners | 2 |
| Apprentice Gardeners | 1 | Butler | 1 |
| Footman | 1 | | |

## TRADESMEN, SHOPKEEPERS AND OTHERS

| | | | |
|---|---|---|---|
| Butchers | 3 | Landowners | 2 |
| Grocers | 2 | Land Agent | 1 |
| Grocer and Flour Seller | 1 | Vicar | 1 |
| Publicans | 4 | Married Women | 98 |
| Joiners | 1 | Children | 203 |
| Blacksmiths | 3 | Widows | 9 |
| Shoemakers | 7 | Retired Men | 3 |
| Unmarried Women and Girls | | Visitors to Spennymoor | 9 |
| At home | 21 | | |

## POPULATION OF WHITWORTH 1851
## FAMILY NAMES AND PLACES OF ORIGIN

| SURNAME | FATHERS PLACE OF BIRTH | MOTHERS PLACE OF BIRTH |
|---|---|---|
| Adams | Northumberland | Newbottle |
| Adamson | Whitworth | Lanchester |
| Adamson | Wolsingham | Wolsingham |
| Alderson | Yorkshire | Yorkshire |
| Bawley | Northumberland | Northumberland |
| Beans | | Ryton |
| Bell | Rushyford | Northumberland |
| Bell | | Shield Row |
| Bell | Ramshaw | Washington |
| Bell | Lambton | Lancashire |

| SURNAME | FATHERS PLACE OF BIRTH | MOTHERS PLACE OF BIRTH |
|---|---|---|
| Bell | Ryton | South Biddick |
| Blewitt | Bishop Auckland | Bishop Auckland |
| Brawley | Northumberland | Jarrow |
| Brown | Northumberland | Fatfield |
| Brown | Scotland | Willington |
| Brown | Lambton | Weardale |
| Buxton | Newcastle | |
| Carter | Heighington | Heighington |
| Cleghorn | Shiney Row | Hetton |
| Cockburn | Heburn | |
| Coulson | Lamesley | Northumberland |
| Crooks | Northumberland | Shiney Row |
| Cutler | Derbyshire | Derbyshire |
| Davies | Wales | Northumberland |
| Davy | Tudhoe | Chester le Street |
| Dickinson | Chester le Street | Northumberland |
| Dobby | Whitworth | Bishop Auckland |
| Dobinson | Yorkshire | Yorkshire |
| Dowson | Newbottle | Cockfield |
| Dunn | Scotland | Scotland |
| Evans | Wales | Wales |
| Evans | Wales | Nottinghamshire |
| Fletcher | Yorkshire | Neasham |
| Forrest | Northumberland | Northumberland |
| Greenwood | Yorkshire | Lancashire |
| Geldart | Yorkshire | West Auckland |
| Gibbon | Heseldon | Brandon |
| Gill | Cumberland | Northumberland |
| Hall | Cockfield | Cockfield |
| Hartley | Lancashire | Lumley |
| Hartley | East Denton | Thorburn |
| Hartley | | Uspeth |
| Harton | Birtley | Washington |
| Heighington | Yorkshire | West Auckland |
| Hetherington | Whitworth | Whitworth |
| Hetherington | Fatfield | Hetton |
| Hodgson | Murton | Ryton |
| Hopper | Yorkshire | Washington |
| Hunter | Northumberland | Ryton |
| Irwin | Houghton le Spring | Easington |
| Johnson | Escombe | Scotland |
| Kirtley | Derbyshire | Yorkshire |
| Langstaff | Yorkshire | Yorkshire |
| Liddle | Gateshead | Northumberland |
| Lonsdale | Sherburn | Jarrow |
| Lonsdale | Tanfield | Chester le Street |
| Mackay | Northumberland | Northumberland |

| SURNAME | FATHERS PLACE OF BIRTH | MOTHERS PLACE OF BIRTH |
|---|---|---|
| McFarlane | Scotland | |
| McGuiness | Scotland | Scotland |
| Minto | Medomsley | Cumberland |
| Minto | Medomsley | Jarrow |
| Minto | Medomsley | Merrington |
| Minto | Medomsley | |
| Newton | Ayton | Northumberland |
| Nicholson | Houghton le Spring | Washington |
| Nicholson | Northumberland | Newcastle |
| Pattison | Whitworth | Whitworth |
| Patrick | Durham City | South Shields |
| Ramshaw | Newcastle | Bishop Auckland |
| Richardson | Lambton | Washington |
| Robinson | Yorkshire | Yorkshire |
| Rowe | Weardale | Hamsterly |
| Shaw | Yorkshire | Cleadon |
| Soulsby | | Northumberland |
| Soulsby | Northumberland | Northumberland |
| Soulsby | Fatfield | |
| Stephenson | Fatfield | |
| Stoves | Penshaw | Penshaw |
| Stratton | Scotland | Nottinghamshire |
| Taylor | Northumberland | Northumberland |
| Tempest | Northumberland | Northumberland |
| Thew | Northumberland | Brancepeth |
| Thornton | Northumberland | Chester le Street |
| Turner | Yorkshire | Yorkshire |
| Walker | Swallwell | Northumberland |
| Walton | Lumley | Birtley |
| Walton | Northumberland | Hetton |
| Walton | Houghton le Spring | |
| White | Hamsterley | |
| Willey | Cowpen | Northumberland |
| Wilson | Sunderland | Shadforth |
| Young | Ryton | Ryton |

## FREEHOLD PROPERTY AT NEW WHITWORTH 1848
### To be sold by auction at the Rose and crown – Durham Market Place

All the newly erected and substantially built Shop Dwelling House and Premises situated at New Whitworth in the County of Durham, at present in the occupation of Mr. Walker, Grocer and Draper. (This would be Joseph Walker who prided himself on being the oldest tradesman in town. See Dodd History of Spennymoor page 132)

The shop faces the Durham and Bishop Auckland road and is well adapted for carrying on an extensive business.

The property consists of Front and Back shop, 6 rooms, cellar, stable and yard; and also a Piece of Building ground adjoining, whereon a small house might be erected….

## COALMINING IN THE SPENNYMOOR AREA.

This is my next project which is already underway. I am looking for any information relating to any of the collieries listed below. I am looking for photographs, anything photographable, maps, plans, any mementos, ephemera and in particular any personal memories or reminiscences of people who worked at any of these collieries or their fathers or grandfathers worked there.

Binchester (Westerton)
Bishops Close
Bowburn
Byers Green
Chilton
Coundon
Croxdale
Fishburn
Leasingthorne
Mainsforth
Metal Bridge Drift
Middlestone Moor Dicky Pit
Middlestone Moor Drift
Merrington Lane + Dicky Pit
Newfield
The Rock Pit
Tudhoe
Tudhoe Grange
Tudhoe Mill Drift
Tursdale
West Cornforth (Thrislington)
Westerton Drift
Whitworth Park
Whitworth Drift